SELLING AND MARKETING FOR SMALL BUSINESSES

BUSINESS GUIDEBOOKS

SELF-HELP GUIDES FOR SMALL BUSINESSMEN

SELLING AND MARKETING FOR SMALL BUSINESSES

DEBORAH FOWLER

SERIES FOREWORD BY DAVID TRIPPIER,
UNDER SECRETARY OF STATE AT THE
DEPARTMENT OF INDUSTRY

Sphere Reference

Sphere Reference
27 Wrights Lane,
London W8 5TZ

First published 1984
Reprinted 1986

Phototypesetting by Megaron Typesetting.

Printed and bound in Great Britain by
Cox & Wyman Ltd, Reading, Berks.

Contents

Series Foreword

by David Trippier MP,
Parliamentary Under Secretary of State for Industry

The environment for small businesses has changed greatly for the better in the past four years. An effective Loan Guarantee Scheme and generous tax relief through the Business Expansion Scheme are only two of many in over 100 Government measures to provide incentives and remove obstacles to business enterprise. Our efforts are complemented by a welcome improvement in attitudes in commerce and industry towards the small business operator.

Vital though these changes are, the success of any new expanding business will always depend on the skill, knowledge and tenacity of those running the firm. Practical sources of expertise and advice, as provided by this series of business Guidebooks, are invaluable aids for the busy entrepreneur. General business management and finance, without doubt, cause the most problems and biggest headaches for the small firm.

Certainly many young businesses have been given a better chance of success by the increasing availability of help with the particular challenges that beset them. I am encouraged by figures which show for the two years, 1981 and 1982, 'births' of new firms well in excess of 'deaths' in spite of the world-wide economic recession.

A flourishing small firms sector in any national economy brings new energy, new enterprise and new initiatives into industry and commerce. These attributes have never been more necessary than in today's tough economic climate and highly competitive world markets. To this end, these business Guidebooks will be a worthwhile investment for every new and expanding business.

Introduction

"I know what I want to do, I know how and where I can do it, I've even got a little money . . . but I don't know how to START."

"Start?" I queried. There was a pause.

"Well, I suppose I mean SELL — I don't know how to *start* selling."

I was in Studio B9 of a local BBC Radio Station somewhere in the heart of the Midlands. I was doing a phone-in — you know the sort of thing, answering people's queries. This time the subject was how to start a small business.

So what was special about this caller? That is the point — NOTHING. He had expressed almost verbatim what the majority of the previous callers had said. It was the same story up and down the country — so many of us believe we have the makings of a good business idea but just do not know how, or where, to start selling it.

Sales are the life-blood of any business, big or small. Without them, there is no business. Viability is a word that the professionals particularly like. "You must demonstrate that your business idea is viable" is a typical bank manager-type pontification. Viable — what does it really mean? Simple — the ability to SELL profitably.

Like so many professions, the function of sales and marketing is shrouded in mystique. We are told that salesmen are born, not made, the suggestion being that selling is a 'closed shop' to the average enthusiast. Many marketing men appear to have lost the ability to speak the Queen's English, jargon has completely taken over.

Selling and marketing is simply a matter of common sense. You can learn to do it just like you can learn to ride a bike. "Ah," you say, "but I *know* I'm not salesman material. I couldn't sell double glazing or insurance, or 'fridges to eskimos." Maybe so, but selling the product or service of your own small business is quite different. It is YOUR baby — YOU created it, YOU believe in it. YOU are its best ambassador.

This book is a step-by-step guide from defining your market through to maximising your selling effort. I am not writing a text book, or preaching a sermon. This publication represents the pooled experiences of myself and my colleagues, and is aimed at giving you the best possible advice on how to SOCK IT TO 'EM!

Let's get started.

To Alan — obviously

Credits

A great many people have helped me with the writing of this book. I would particularly like to thank:

British Overseas Trade Board
Department of Industry — Small Firms Division
Alan Fowler
Douglas Hamilton
Hotchkiss Kruger Associates
Viola Niness
Tom Parker (deceased)
John Runacres
Arnold Wayne

Section 1.   Marketing

Marketing is a two-tier process.

Firstly, it is terribly important that before starting your business, you carefully define your market. The term used is MARKET RESEARCH, and, contrary to popular belief, it does not need to be an amazingly scientific, nor even a particularly time consuming process. There are plenty of short cuts.

Market Research is a vital requirement, however, for starting any business and in this section I will take you through the various questions you need to ask yourself before you begin trading. You think you have a wonderful business idea, so does your mother and your best friend . . . but you all may be wrong. Your idea only has merit if you have potential customers out there somewhere wanting what you have got. Time spent in market research is time well spent. Repenting at leisure, with shelves full of obsolete stock, is no joke.

The second function of marketing is to act as a continuing back-up to the selling effort. In other words, not so much MARKETING as MONITORING. Just because you have found a market for your product or service, it does not mean you have 'made it'. Your thinking needs to be constantly updated in all aspects of your field of operation.

Whether you are starting a business or actually running one, being alert to market trends will take you a long way down the road towards success.

1. What's It All About?

The importance of Market Research and where to start.

If I said to you "why not buy this fantastic car of mine, it is an absolute bargain", what would your reaction be? You would say you wanted to know more about it first. You would test drive it, you would look under the bonnet, check the bodywork for rust and study the miles on the clock. You might well take the car to your local garage for a second opinion. Then . . . and only then, would you make me an offer.

This is the sort of attitude you would normally apply to any large purchase where you are committing a considerable sum of money. If you are intending to start your own small business in all probability you will not only be committing money, but that most valuable commodity of all – your time. Yet indications are that many first-time businessmen undertake very little detailed analysis as to their chances of success before taking the plunge – in many cases far less than if they were buying a new family car.

Good ideas can be said to be 'two a penny'. Putting them into action is quite another matter. You may be able to offer what you consider to be a good product, or service; you may have sufficient capital to launch it, premises from which to operate it, a trustworthy partner or staff to help you, and the technical know-how necessary. But the million dollar question is – DOES ANYONE WANT WHAT YOU HAVE TO OFFER?

The following check list asks the kind of questions that you must ask yourself before making any firm commitments towards starting your own business.

1. Is your product or service good enough to get the edge on your competitors? If not, it may need amending, and remember this is not just a comparison of the commodity itself, but also its reliability, price, quality and your delivery performance.

2. The all important question – you need to analyse the size of the market. Are there sufficient people out there who want what you have to offer?

3. What is the long term future of your business? Is it a 'seven day wonder' – if so can your ideas be adapted to keep pace with changing trends?

    N.B.   There is nothing wrong with taking advantage of a 'seven day wonder', so long as you recognise it as such and know when to get out.

4. Are you really providing what the *buyer* wants? You need to recognize the difference between customer and buyer.

5. Pricing – On the one hand, will your customer be prepared to pay the price you have to charge in order to make a profit, and on the other, are you charging enough?

6. Then there are the practicalities which may or may not apply to your particular business idea; have you the right location, the right premises, the right staff, the right machinery, the right stock levels and the right production time – not just to ensure the smooth

running of your business but in order to appeal to your customer?

7. Can you present what you have to offer in the right way? Does your business have the right image?

8. How accessible is your customer? He may be there all right, but can you get at him without large cash resources or a big organisation behind you?

In the following chapters, we will look at each of these questions in turn. As you answer each one in relation to your own business, you will be in fact formulating your own marketing plan. By the end of this first section, your market research programme will be complete.

So where do we begin? The place to start is with the competition. Before deciding how you will approach your market you need to find out what everyone else is doing. Many people believe that in order to go into business they need an original idea. Every decade or so the country throws up an entrepreneur whose brilliant invention revolutionizes some small part of our civilisation. But for every one like him, there are thousands and thousands of successful businessmen who are offering, in all major respects, what their competitors are offering — differing only in details such as location, size, quality, price and colour.

The value of carefully assessing the competition is two-fold. On the one hand you can learn from their successes and failures — in other words the areas where you should emulate them, and those to which you should give a wide berth. All right, let us call it by its correct name — industrial espionage! On the other hand, it is a question of assessing your competitors' grip on the market, to see whether there is room for you and your business as well as theirs. Let us look at these two aspects in more detail.

1. *Industrial espionage.* I am not a great believer in higher education unless the business of your choice requires you to have a high degree of technical skill. If you are considering going into business in an area in which you are neither trained nor have direct experience, then in my view the best way to gain a good, solid, working knowledge of the market, is to go and work for the competition. It does not matter how humble the job, you can still keep your ears and eyes open.

Supposing, for example, you receive some redundancy money and decided to buy a little news agency business. On the face of it the business feels familiar. We all have a little news agency in our life, which we visit on a regular basis — surely, it is just a question of keeping the right stocks of magazines, newspapers, sweets and tobacco? As any retailer will tell you, it is not that simple. The right balance of stock, weighed against the right balance of gross profit is vital in order to make a living, and an awful lot of people

5

go wrong. I would strongly recommend if you are considering any form of retailing, that first you go and work in a shop and learn the ropes; and what applies to retailing, applies to every sort of business — from running a marriage bureau to manufacturing ball bearings. Your period of self-imposed training does not need to be very lengthy, unless your chosen business is highly technical. You just need to assimilate everything that is going on.

This advice could be said to be not particularly moral, but it is practical. What matters to me is that YOU launch a successful business. *Learning from other people's mistakes is free. Learning from your own can cost you your livelihood.*

2. *Can you compete?* In assessing the strength of the competition, the factors worthy of consideration will obviously vary enormously from business to business. If you are manufacturing a product for a selected market, your distribution may well be nation-wide, in which case your location may not be of primary concern. If, however, you are offering a service, or anticipating some form of retail business, location is everything. There is little point in opening a fish and chip shop in your home town if it already sports three, and a couple of Chinese take-aways!

Look carefully at your competitors' strengths and weaknesses. Weaknesses can be exploited, strengths can be copied. But how, you may say? I cannot simply walk into their premises and ask them how they run their business. Yes you can, more or less. You have GOT to be ruthless if you are going into business. It is the jungle out there and as in all jungles, only the toughest will survive. If it is a competitors' product in which you are interested, buy one, rent one, lease one, borrow one, but learn everything you can about it. If it is a service, try it out for yourself.

My husband, Alan, and I, recently advised a young man who wanted to start a business hiring out a Rolls Royce for weddings and other such functions. He was unmarried, but we instantly voted him a fictitious fiancée and sent him round all the car hire firms to obtain quotations and full details for his pending nuptials. His findings told him a lot. Firstly, where to pitch his price — not too low, not too high. Secondly, and this was an important factor, the other car hire firms in his particular area, were all affiliated to large motor distributors, and therefore extremely impersonal. He, therefore, slanted all his advertising and sales material towards a very personal approach, which stood him in sharp contrast to his competitors. Thirdly, living in a tourist area, he established that none of his competitors offered their cars for tourist trips, so he immediately contacted the Tourist

Board. The result is he runs an extremely successful business, driving Americans round the Cotswolds during the week, and brides to the church on time at weekends.

Do be discriminating, however, in assessing competitors' shortcomings. Do not simply assume that because no one has manufactured say, 'sky-blue widgets' that the market is wide open for you. There may be a very good reason why no one has, and it is very dangerous to assume that a market is automatically available to you because the competition has been too short-sighted to attack it. Retail outlets are a prime example of this. I am sure in your local town you have seen certain sites where shop after shop has opened, only to close a few months later. Presumably each new retailer thinks he knows where the previous trader went wrong, and feels he can do better. But it is probably not the retail operation at all that is at fault. Probably it will be something to do with the premises being unwelcoming or simply in the wrong place. So be warned — do not assume your competitor is a fool, though if he is, so much the better!

Market Research is a step-by-step operation. Only when you have thoroughly assessed the competition and feel confident that you can stand shoulder to shoulder with them, should you then turn your attention to how you can beat . . . or, indeed, join them.

2. Who's There?

How to assess the size of your market potential.

The commodity you have to sell may be aimed at the mass market, or it may have largely specialist appeal.

On the face of it, the mass market seems easier to tackle. Surely the more people who want what you have to offer, the better. But remember, the bigger the market, the bigger the competition. Finding the right market for a specialist item may be more difficult initially, but once you have it identified you may well find selling to it a great deal easier than the more competitive areas.

Finding a specialist market is a question of breaking down and discarding those elements of the market-place which are of no use to you, or your business. Supposing, for example, you designed a gadget which, when clamped to bannisters, helped old and disabled people to climb stairs. The first stage of your market research would be to simply ascertain the number of old and disabled people in the country. Stage two would be to assess how many of these people live in special residential homes and therefore do not require your gadget. Stage three would be to assess how many old and disabled people live in bungalows or flats (a much higher percentage than the rest of the population). Stage four would be a question of estimating the number of people who, though occupying houses, have already made their living quarters on the ground floor, and have no requirement to go upstairs. You see what I am getting at? It is not enough to simply identify the total size of the potential market. You then have to take that figure and break it down, stage by stage, until you are left with the essential element that is relevant to your business. You may well find that what started out as a huge market, in fact, may be very small indeed.

It is a difficult balancing act. If your product or service has too wide an appeal, you may well find the competition enormous − if on the other hand, your product or service is too specialist, your potential market may prove too small a base on which to launch a viable business.

So how do you assess whether the size of your intended market is large enough to warrant your entry into it? By asking yourself this question − MY CUSTOMER − WHO IS HE, WHERE IS HE, WHY IS HE? It is difficult to generalize sufficiently to cover all aspects of business life, and I think the best way I can demonstrate how you should answer this question for yourself, is to offer a series of examples.

Who is he?

Let us pursue, by way of example, the gadget for helping the elderly and disabled upstairs. Breaking down the market in the way I suggested was simply a mental exercise, using your own common sense. Now you need to put the flesh on the bones − you need some facts and figures to substantiate your beliefs. In the case of this particular project, I would assume that you are already in touch with charitable organizations, such as Help The Aged, since, presumably, the gadget would need to have been thoroughly tested for design perfection and safety. These organizations would be able to help you establish, firstly, what percentage of the population are actually old or disabled, and then what percentage of those people had any real need for your gadget. From the information they provided, you would be able to assess whether there were 2,000, 20,000 or 200,000 people out there who would benefit from what you have to offer. Of course, the next stage is to establish how you reach them and what price they would be prepared to pay, but long before you start looking at those aspects, you need to ascertain just how big a market potential there is. You cannot start manufacturing an item which you can only ever sell to five hundred people unless your unit selling price runs into thousands of pounds.

The thinking process I have suggested for stair climbing gadgets applies to every other form of business. Here is another example which demonstrates what I mean. A few months ago I had a letter from a lady who wanted to open a Nigerian restaurant. She had a number of detailed questions, but the major query was — "Is it a good idea?"

Although we British are fairly conventional about our food, we are gradually learning to be more adventurous, and on the face of it, a Nigerian restaurant sounded a very good idea. The problem with her plan, in my view, was that she was intending opening the restaurant in Weybridge, Surrey. Weybridge is not a large place, and I asked her what percentage of the population she thought would be interested in a Nigerian restaurant. She had no idea, but said that her cousin was running a very successful restaurant along the same lines in Earls Court. I am not surprised. Earls Court is the heart of London bedsitter land, with many, many, more people per square foot than Weybridge — young people mostly, cosmopolitan, always ready to try something new. I am sure her cousin is making a fortune. But what chances in Weybridge. . . ?

My suggestion to her was that she opened her restaurant with *some* Nigerian dishes, but that she should also have a good selection of English or French recipes on the menu, for maximum appeal. But that will run the risk of watering down her image, you may say. Well, perhaps it will, but I think it is the best way to 'hedge her bets' — she can always increase the Nigerian dishes, if they prove popular.

In assessing your market, you must maintain flexibility of mind. You do need to tailor-make your product or service to your customers' requirements. My lady with her Nigerian restaurant, is stuck with Weybridge. She has to live there because of family commitments. Therefore, in my view she should provide what the inhabitants of Weybridge are most likely to want, rather than automatically assume that a successful formula in Earls Court can be repeated in Surrey.

This, of course, brings us to location. . . .

Where is he?

Are you going to offer your product or service nationally . . . or locally?

Supposing for example, you have worked for some years in a large retail chain store, which operates nationally. You could take advantage of your expertise and knowledge by opening your own small retail outlet, aimed at appealing to a local population, whose shopping facilities are perhaps somewhat limited. From your global knowledge of the country, providing what people want in a single locality should be something you are well able to do, and should be very successful.

The reverse can equally well apply. Supposing you work for a marine engineers in Portsmouth, and while doing so, let us say you design an excellent self-starter for use with outboard engines. Having developed the technique, you decide to launch out on your own, open a little workshop and market your product. Up to that point, working with the marine engineers would have meant your customers were locally based, but you cannot rely on these people alone to buy your self-starter. You need to be convinced that you can sell your product nationally, in order to be sure of a viable business.

The importance of location varies enormously from business to business. Obviously for retail outlets and services to the consumer, it is vital — if you are a freight forwarder, you need to be based at Heathrow — our marine engineer is not going to be very successful in Worcester. These are obvious examples, but in a surprising number of cases, location can prove to be the key factor. Having identified who your customer is, it may well be that you can score over the competition by being closer to him, or winkling him out in places which other people have not bothered to explore, which brings us to. . . .

Why is he?

WHY someone is likely to become your customer is best looked at, in the vast majority of cases, by making a comparison between yourself and your competitor — as indeed outlined in the previous chapter. In some instances, of course, you may attract customers because you have developed something entirely new, but in the vast majority of businesses, you attract customers because one element of your business venture is different from that of your competitors. You do not need necessarily to be *better*, you just need to place a different emphasis on the qualities of your product or service.

Another way of establishing a market could be to find new applications for an existing type of business. In other words, you do not need to change fundamentally the product or service already being offered. Instead you find a new market outlet. Surely one of the most successful examples of this, are jeans. Levi Strauss were making jeans when the first covered wagons rolled across the plains of America. A hundred years later, someone had the bright idea that generations of cowboys had really looked rather good in jeans, and that perhaps here was a fashion idea. Of course over the years jeans have changed. They have now been made for women as well as men, in stretch denim and corduroy, but the fashion market was established with the original western-style jean . . . and the rest, as they say, is history.

So it is a question of looking out for an unusual application of an existing item. I am told that in The States, one of the smartest ways to serve chips is in a Victorian chamber pot. Someone must have made an absolute fortune exporting these and building up a cult!

Alternatively it may be possible to broaden your customer potential by slightly varying the style of a particular service or product. Here computers must be the prime example. Computers were originally developed as a scientific tool, then an industrial one. With the introduction of the microchip, not only did computers become commercially viable in small offices and shops, but also in the home, and in the toy industry. I bet those original pioneers would have been astounded to be told that their brain child could be seen represented today by a £4.99 toy in a child's Christmas stocking. Yes, they knew computers had an enormous future and were likely to revolutionize the industrial world . . . but a toy?

This, of course, is an extreme example, but you may well find that some small change of emphasis in your business approach could open up a whole new world for you.

In conclusion, therefore, ask yourself this question. What are you trying to achieve in terms of market share? It has to be the maximum number of potential customers balanced against the extent of the competition. By 'extent of the competition', I mean that there are some areas where the competition is so high it is virtually a closed shop, and by contrast, areas where although there is a great deal of competition, there is still room for the small businessman to sneak the few customers necessary to give himself a toehold. Of course there are many other factors to be taken into account when finally assessing your ultimate market potential, but in this chapter I am concerned only with 'could be' i.e. you need to establish the number of customers who 'could be' interested in what you have to offer. Once we know that, we can then study how the various other factors will influence this figure, one way or the other.

3.   Have I Backed a Winner?

The importance of recognizing the future for your business.

GOOD   IDEA ... BAD TIMING

"Eve, darling, I have just invented this marvellous thing—
it's called a contraceptive pill."

Commerce in the 1980's is not easy. Things change so fast – today's bright idea can be 'old hat' tomorrow. Has your business idea got a long term future, or if not, are you aware of its life-span? Don't misunderstand me, in no way am I criticising the concept of taking advantage of a fashionable trend, so long as you recognize it for what it is. People have made fortunes from a quick in-out deal, but jumping on the bandwagon and off again, at just the right moment, takes considerable skill.

One of the most obvious examples of a craze that made money for a few but cost a fortune to many, is skate-boarding. Children in this country had a momentary obsession with the sport, but everyone took it too seriously instead of recognizing it for what it was. Manufacturing units were set up, whole retail outlets established, newspapers and magazines started – even Local Authorities up and down the country started building skate-board parks, many of which, even today, lie derelict. It was all over in a matter of months, and with it, many companies went to the wall. Do not fall into the same sort of trap.

There are so many factors which can affect your potential market. Here is a check list of the primary areas you should watch.

1. *Market trends.*

    Obviously, if the business of your choice involves any form of high fashion, or is a craze such as skate-boarding – watch out. Not so obvious, but potentially just as deadly, is a declining market. You need to establish whether your particular industry is in a state of growth or decline, because even a drop in the market of 1% could easily put you out of business.

    Take bread, which is a declining market, since we all became so obsessed with slimming. If you were considering starting your own bakery, probably you would be completely safe if you are the only baker for miles around, with as many customers as you can handle. You can afford a slow decline in the market. If on the other hand you are just another baker in a large town, you might have enough customers now, but it would be sensible to keep an eye on the future. Perhaps you could hive off part of the shop to sell health foods, such as brown rice and wholemeal flour. Perhaps you could try and win one or two outside catering contracts to supply, say, bread rolls to your local hospital. Perhaps you could try selling quiches as well as cream cakes. Whatever you do in these circumstances, you must recognize that declining market and seek ways of side-stepping it to avoid a loss of turnover. Dare I say it, "use your loaf"!

    How do you establish whether you are in a growth or declining area, if you do not already know? Trade magazines are your best bet, or talking to the competition. Advertising and media men can also be useful, since they should have their finger on the pulse of developing trends — but do not hire them, just pick their brains.

Beware of local trends. A market might be in the state of overall decline in the country as a whole, but in your particular area, it may be holding its own, or vice versa.

Beware too of temporary trends. A temporary boost in demand can be very dangerous. You may start committing yourself to extra machinery, extra staff, bigger premises, only to find that the bubble bursts. Similarly, it is sensible not to panic at a sudden decline. It could so easily be a temporary factor, caused by outside influences, which will soon pass.

2. *Government legislation*

I can hear you groaning, but sorry, you have got to work your way through this one. Monopolies, wage restraints, embargoes, environmental changes, factory acts — all these factors can have a devastating effect on your business, if there is a sudden change at the wrong time. You do need to keep abreast with what is going on. With specific enquiries, your Local Government Office should be able to help, but in terms of general information, I would discuss any likely problem areas with your bank manager and/or your accountant, both of whom should be thoroughly versed in the horrors of bureaucracy.

Conversely, the introduction of new legislation can open up business opportunities for you. A tightening of the Factory Acts would be very welcome if you are in the fire extinguisher business, so keep alert.

3. *Local Factors.*

Here I am thinking primarily of development, good and bad. You need to be aware of plans for motorways, ring roads, housing and shop developments. "Ah," you say, "these things do not affect me, I am not a retailer, I am in light engineering". Possibly you are right, and yet the new motorway access that is to be built only two hundred yards from your factory might, on the one hand, double your rent, and on the other improve your distribution. Both side-effects could have a tremendous effect on your business.

If you are to run a successful business, you need to know what is going on in your local area. With specific enquiries your Local Planning Officer can help you, and keep reading the local papers. They can prove invaluable.

4. *Practical considerations.*

It is difficult to generalize here, but whilst there may be nothing wrong with your market — i.e. people are going to go on wanting what you produce — it may be that the method by which you produce it is doomed. Perhaps you know in the long term there is only a limited supply of raw materials, or perhaps the service you are offering is soon to be updated by technology. Either way, if you know that, for whatever reason, you will not be able to trade in the same style in the long term, you need to very carefully amortize your capital costs over a short period to make sure you can afford to be in business at all.

Take a service industry, as an example. If today I decided that I was going to start a bureau supplying secretarial services, I would not buy a duplicating machine. I would buy a word processor. A duplicating machine, second-hand, today, would probably cost £150, whereas a good-quality word processor is somewhere nearer £2,000 or £3,000. But I would have to look to the future. In the long term, those messy duplicated letters are simply not going to be acceptable to my potential customers. They will want neat, high-quality work, that looks as though it has been typed by an individual. The purchase of a duplicator would be a false economy.

These, therefore, are a few factors which I hope you will find helpful in assessing your business's future. It is your capital costs you particularly have to watch. Never make a large investment in anything − whether it is property, machinery, manpower, or your own valuable time, unless you truly believe that in the long term there is a market there, which will justify the expenditure.

The alternative to careful planning for the future is, of course, 'the fast buck'. We all dream of it, don't we? The one deal that will really put us on the map − wipe out the overdraft, the mortgage, and the HP commitments, and leave us planning our holidays in the Bahamas. These deals are still around, even in today's difficult climate, but, by goodness, you have to be very sure of your facts.

We have a friend who tells a very good story against himself to illustrate this point. He is an extremely successful businessman and his particular field is engineering. Engineering is what he knows and understands, but being a natural wheeler dealer, he cannot resist the odd little dabble on the side. Some years ago, a shoe manufacturer from Hong Kong approached him. His company was in trouble and he had 50,000 pairs of beautifully-made leather shoes, which he had to off-load fast, at a fraction of their correct price, in order to stay solvent. Our friend could not resist the deal. He took the shoes home to his wife who confirmed that they were beautiful, and had a retail potential of eight or nine times the price being asked. Our friend went ahead . . . how could he fail? He did, because the one factor that he had not checked out was that these shoes were originally made for the Chinese market, and as we all know, Chinese feet are tiny compared with ours. The shoes he received were all in sizes one, two and three, whereas the average British woman's shoe size is five. How stupid, you say, he deserved what happened to him, he should have checked it out more carefully. I agree, but then he did not know anything about shoes, and that is the danger. My advice is, do not dabble in 'flash-in-the-pan' markets, unless it is an area in which you have had a great deal of experience. Large scale fortunes are usually made as a result of large scale experience. There are very few short cuts.

So there you have it. If you are considering making any long term commitment, thoroughly explore your business idea — locally, regionally and nationally. Look at its long term future from every angle and do not commit yourself too heavily in areas which may be subject to change. And if you are going to try your luck on a quick in-and-out venture . . . well, good luck!

4.   Who's Who?

Who is your buyer, who is your customer − can you recognize the difference?

Concentrate on selling to your buyer − let him worry about the end user.

For many small businesses the difference between buyer and customer is immaterial — because there is none. Whether you are selling a product or a service, in many cases the person to whom you sell is in fact the consumer. Perhaps you make pine furniture which you sell through a craft shop of your own. Perhaps you sell your services as a freelance accountant. Perhaps you run a restaurant, or a village shop — in all these cases you have one major influence in your life, your customer or your client — and it is your job to please them, and provide what they want.

However, business is not always that simple. Supposing you make a toy car for your son. He and his friends love it so much that you decide to go into business manufacturing toy cars. You cannot sell a single product from your own retail outlet, so you need to sell through other people's. Suddenly you do not have one customer any more, you have three — the buyer working for the retail outlet, the child's parent or friend who is going to make the purchase, and the child himself. Pleasing the child is one thing, and a very important factor of which you must not lose sight, but you also have to please the buyer, and the purchaser. Just because your son loves the car you have made, it does not mean that the buyer for a chain store will also. Your car may be statistically too big, too expensive, blue instead of red, and to cap it all, fall short of Health and Safety standards.

Perhaps, by contrast, you have been a draughtsman for some years and have never really worked at what you consider to be a satisfactory drawing board. You design one for yourself — it is perfect. You show it to one or two of your colleagues and they think it is splendid too, and ask you to make them one. Suddenly you have the makings of a business — producing drawing boards which draughtsmen really like. But how are you going to sell your drawing board? You have to find a number of office equipment retail outlets, who are prepared to sell them for you. If you find resistance from the buyers of these outlets — they consider your drawing board too expensive, too cumbersome, or whatever, then sadly, however good your idea, it is a non-starter.

The lesson here is that there is an understandable tendency for us to concentrate solely on the end user, rather than the people in between. Buyers are highly professional people, usually with a wealth of statistics at their fingertips. The buyer of Selfridges may well know that he simply cannot sell an electric toaster over £14.99, however good it is. Therefore it is pointless your producing a wildly sophisticated one, which he will have to sell for £30.

I think it is also worth making a point here that timing is a critical factor. If you have a wonderful idea for a revolutionary new snorkel, on the face of it, Spring should be the best time to launch your business. Not so, unless you yourself are selling direct to the public. Most buyers — and

19

this applies whether you are talking wholesale, retail or mail order — plan their buying at least nine months ahead. Charging into Lilliwhites in the first week of March, clutching your snorkel, is likely to excite the response that if you were selling ski boots, they might be interested.

Remember — the customer is the person who pays the bill.

Do not close your mind to alterations or amendments to your product or service, in your preparation for marketing it. Take your prototype along to a potential buyer as soon as you can, and ask his advice. Do not waste money manufacturing stock of something which could be totally unsuitable from a marketing point of view, albeit that the end user appears satisfied with it. Be flexible, listen to what buyers tell you and be influenced by what they say. There is many a pioneer who has gone to the wall through persisting with the development of a brilliant idea, which none the less is totally uncommercial.

But you say, I know my idea is good and I simply cannot find a buyer who will even look at it. What do I do, give up? No, not necessarily, there are ways, of course, for a manufacturer/innovator to sell direct to the user — by mail order or by opening his own shop. Habitat is an excellent case in point. Terence Conran had the idea that furniture needed a complete face-lift. It needed to be stylish, practical and cheap. It needed a new look, simple clear lines, fresh bright colours. Could he sell the concept to furniture stores? He could not. No one wanted to know. He did not give up though. He opened his own shop and Habitat was born, but he took a big risk.

I am not saying that professional buyers know all the answers and are always right, but they do have their finger on the pulse when it comes to assessing their (and your) customers' requirements.

So if *your* buyer and *the* customer is not the same person you are going to have to learn to please them both!

5. What is the Price of Success?

Pitching your prices right — you can as easily be too cheap as too expensive.

It is tempting to believe that the quick way to break into a market is to undercut the prices of the competition. Everyone else is selling widgets from between 19p and 20p each, so you offer your widgets at 18p. It may *sound* the easy way, but it is also the most dangerous and, frankly, not to be recommended.

Let us look at the disadvantages. Firstly, if you are successful in obtaining orders for your 18p widget, you are going to have a serious impact on your competitors' business. They are not just going to sit back and let you walk off with their sales, they will drop their price to 18p as well, and suddenly you are in the midst of a price war. What are you going to do then, go down to 17p? Bear in mind that in any price war, your competitors are far more likely to win than you are. They have been in the trade longer than you. They probably have past profits to live off while they sell unprofitable widgets in order to put you out of business.

Secondly, price cutting for its own sake does not impress your buyer. In most instances buyers are looking for far more than simply the cheapest commodity around. They want regular supply, reliable delivery and consistent good quality. Their immediate reaction will be that you will not be able to maintain this cheaper price. You will either go out of business, or sooner or later, put the price up to match that of your competitors. It is true to say that buyers view price cutting with deep suspicion and they are right to do so.

Thirdly, why is everyone else selling widgets at between 19p and 20p? Answer – because at 19p or 20p they are making a profit. Remember the profit that counts is not simply the difference between your buying (or manufacturing) price and your selling price – first you have to deduct your overheads. An order for 20,000 widgets at 20p is far more valuable than an order for 50,000 at 10p. Your competitors will have pitched their price as a result of a careful costing exercise. It is possible that you might be able to make your widgets cheaper, but far more likely your business will just go to the wall.

What applies to widgets and manufacturing applies to every trade. If you open up a Fast Food restaurant and sell your hamburgers at 35p when everyone else is selling them at 55p, you will not attract more trade. People will just think you have used horsemeat – and they will probably be right. Consumers are increasingly aware of value for money. The cheapest item on the shelf will not be the highest seller, particularly where quality is likely to vary.

It is *clever* pricing, not *under*pricing, which will help you compete in the market-place. Here are some golden rules:

1. Offer goods or services at the same price as your competitors but convince your customer you are offering better quality.
2. Offer goods or services at the same price as your competitors, but offer them something extra – fast delivery, a wider choice of colours or sizes, or better presentation.
3. Offer goods or services at a higher price and a higher comparable

standard, and convince your customer that they should think upmarket.

4. Offer goods or services at a lower price, not by comparing like-with-like with your competitors, but by offering a modified version of whatever is currently on the market. In other words they get less, but they pay less.

5. Finally, when pricing, do not under-value your business. New businessmen, particularly, have a tendency to under-rate their achievements. Remember your business is probably at least as good as everyone else's − think positive.

Pricing, like everything else, is subject to trends. The more an item is in demand, the more you can charge for it. Learn to judge your market fluctuations and react accordingly. Above all, do not be hidebound by what the item you have to sell originally cost you. Sell whatever you have to offer at the highest possible price you can demand for it, irrespective of its cost to you. You are a small businessman, trying to earn a living to stay afloat in difficult times. Do not, whatever you do, feel guilty about making excessive profits − you will have your lean times too. If there are rich pickings to be had, take them.

Having advised you not to look at pruning your price as a way to conquering a market, it is equally unrealistic not to recognize that pricing can very often be a deciding factor in whether you do, or do not, make a sale. All I have really said is that it is wrong to use price as your only weapon.

A friend of mine, some years ago, used to work for Clive Sinclair, the electronics genius, at the time he had just developed, and made his first million from selling desk top calculators. He was bubbling over with new ideas for developing his range of calculators, but was uncertain in which direction to move in order to take best advantage of the market. He asked my friend to do a quick market research programme for him, to ascertain the way ahead. My friend had just one week, hardly enough time to brief market research consultants, let alone put them to work. He took the initiative himself and rang round every major stationery store, asked to speak to the buyer and then asked his views as to how he would like to see the calculator develop.

It was astounding. The response was unanimous. What everybody wanted was not greater sophistication, smarter or more elaborate machines. What the buyers wanted was a machine that would sell for under £15. A calculator that could be used in the home and in the office − it did not need to be complicated, it needed to be cheap. It is another case of where history finishes the story − the cheap calculator is now in every home. It is now a part of everyday life. Why − because the price is right, but then so is the product.

The moral of this tale is that you cannot look at price in isolation. You cannot expect to undercut a market and get away with it. Vary the product, vary the service and apply the appropriate price accordingly, up or down, and suddenly . . . you are in business.

6. Have You Bitten Off More Than You Can Chew?

Realize the importance to your business of back-up services.

When formulating a marketing plan, it is essential to look beyond the merits of the commodity you have to offer. You also must have the back-up facilities available to offer your customer. What do I mean by back-up facilities? Here is a check list:

Financial resources
Production capacity/production turn-round
Storage capacity
Suitable premises and equipment
Distribution
Staffing levels

Let us take a look at these elements, one by one:

1. *Financial resources.*

Ask any receiver or liquidator, and they will tell you that most small businesses go bankrupt as a direct result of over-trading. What do we mean by over-trading? It means trading at a rate in excess of your cash resources. It cannot make sense in the long term to accept a large order which you know you will not be able to fund from the cash you have available. It can only mean that you will let your customer down, which in turn means no more orders from him, and the beginnings of a reputation for unreliability. There are very often ways round this situation. If you can extract a written contract from your customer, and your bank manager considers him to be a good financial risk, you can probably borrow money against that contract in order to fulfil the order. Alternatively, your customer may be prepared to give you a payment on account, in order to allow you to fund the costs involved.

Either way, if you are accepting an order which will stretch your cash resources, do be careful. It is so tempting in the early days to clutch at any straw. The new businessman is so grateful that anybody wants to place an order, it is easy to get carried away on a tide of euphoria without doing enough careful thinking. If you are committing a large amount of capital to a single project, do make sure of your customer's credit worthiness. If your customer went into liquidation in these circumstances, so would you.

2. *Production capacity and turn-round.*

Most entrepreneurs are prepared to work day and night in order to fulfil a panic order, and this stands them in very good stead. It is this kind of personal service which helps the small businessman score over the large one. If you are building your business on a reputation for reliability and personal service, however, do be careful not to over-stretch yourself. It is so easily done, and whilst in the short term it might make one month's turnover look better, in the long term it can lose you a great deal of business.

Make sure when approaching your customer that you have already worked out your production levels, and if you find they are not adequate, then tell your customer so. He may well be able to re-schedule his requirements and he will appreciate your honesty.

On the other hand, you must not lose sight of the fact that production capacity is an integral part of the product itself. If your production capabilities are not adequate to meet the majority of your customer's requirements, essentially it means your business idea is non-viable.

This sort of thinking applies to all types of business. If you are opening a shop or restaurant, do not be over-optimistic about the number of hours you can stay open, or indeed the number of hours that you personally can stand behind the counter, or wait at table. In planning at what price you will mark up the dresses you are going to sell in your dress shop, you need to bear in mind that you are going to have to ask, say, Joan to work Monday mornings, and all day Wednesday for you, in order to allow you time to get out and do the buying.

Freelance service is another area fraught with problems when it comes to 'production capacity'. Most freelance people will tell you — whether they are journalists, artists, accountants, secretaries, or whatever — that they are always in 'a chicken and egg' situation. They either do not have enough work, and they are worried sick about paying the rent, or they have too much work, and they are worried sick about letting down their clients. The problem is that as a freelancer, the moment you start letting down your clients, you are finished. So if you are offering freelance services and you know that taking on another client will leave you with no free time at all, do not just hope you can manage, go through the exercise of taking on extra help. Look very carefully at how you spend every day. It could be that extra help is not something which need be directly connected with your business. A part-time gardener, child minder, cleaner, or typist, could give you that extra ten hours a week, which would mean that you could take on one more client.

Whatever type of business you are in, BE REALISTIC about your production capacity.

3. *Storage capacity.*

This is an important factor, whether you are manufacturing car components or quiche lorraines. Too much stock is another of the main contributors to business failure. Equally, however, in certain industries, if you are to provide the back-up service a customer requires, you must have stock. Try and keep your stocking levels realistic and under control. Sit down and work out the value of the stock you already have or will require. Imagine it is money in the bank on which you could be receiving interest. The loss of potential revenue can be quite frightening. Stock represents dead money. Far better, if you can, make your production fast and efficient, and keep your stocking levels at an absolute minimum. When talking to potential customers, try and initially quote delivery dates which will allow you to produce from scratch, rather than supply from stock.

4. *Premises.*

This is a very wide area. As we have already discussed in previous chapters, if you are in any form of retail business, location is everything. Get it wrong, and your business fails. The right premises, however, are important to all forms of business. From your own experience, you will know that you can operate so much more efficiently in pleasant surroundings. Aim to find premises in which you feel happy working, and if you have staff, bear in mind, the better the premises, the more work you will get from them.

Premises are very important from a customer's point of view. Customers are easily impressed by smart, clean, efficient-looking premises − premises do not need to be luxurious, in fact quite the contrary. (If a customer sees too much money spent on your premises, he will probably think you are overcharging!) If on the other hand, a customer sees an air of general chaos, as he walks around, it will seriously undermine your chances of obtaining an order.

5. *Distribution.*

Distribution is a very important factor. In the next section of this book, we will be exploring distribution in detail. Sufficient to say here, that your product or service is of no use to you, or your customers, unless you can find the right way of reaching them.

6. *Staffing.*

The hire of staff should be a carefully planned event – it has to be these days. The high degree of legislation which surrounds staff, makes it very difficult once you have got them, to get rid of them. It is very much a case of "hire in haste and repent in leisure". Do not be panicked into taking on extra staff the moment orders start to flow in. It might well be better to turn down a few orders, and service the rest from existing staff, than rush into something which might only prove a temporary bulge.

If your business allows for it, hiring staff on a contract basis is a good idea. Supposing you are a public relations consultant, operating on your own – suddenly a marvellous opportunity comes up. A major company in consumer goods wants you to launch a short, sharp campaign for them, to promote a brand new product. You cannot do it alone – you must have help. In this case, hire an extra pair of hands for, say, three months of the campaign, on the understanding that their period of employment is linked to the period of the promotion. If you find at the end of three months, your business is doing so well that you can keep on your extra member of staff, so much the better for both of you, but there is no commitment to do so.

Back-up facilities have to be looked at in two ways:

1. You need them to be right in order to make your product or service attractive to the market-place. In this context, when you are learning all you can about your competitors' businesses, learn about their back-up services as well. You have to be able to compete on all levels – you cannot look at your product or service in isolation.

2. Against that, do not be forced into a position where you are stretching your back-up services to a point where it will jeopardize your business.

Case study

For many years I have worked in textiles. It is a well known fact in our trade, that one major chain store (who will be nameless, to avoid giving my solicitor a heart attack!) has been responsible for bankrupting literally hundreds of small British clothing manufacturers. Their policy is this. They find a manufacturer, who is producing, or can produce, exactly what they want. The group is sufficiently large, that within a matter of weeks they tend to use up all the manufacturer's capacity. Orders flood in and, understandably, he cannot resist them. He buys extra machines, takes on extra staff, builds an extension onto his factory . . . and then the fashion passes. The chain store in question has no qualms, no feelings of guilt. They simply move out and on to the next manufacturer, who is providing the latest fashion trend. What happens to the man who is left behind, with all his extra equipment and staff? Nine times out of ten, he goes out of business.

A salutary lesson — it is YOU who should be running your business, not your customer.

7. Are You What You Seem?

A guide to image building.

'See yourself as others see you' — it is a useful phrase in any context, but particularly so when it comes to a careful appraisal of your own business aspirations. Your business image is very important, and how you project it can affect enormously your achievements in the market.

This may sound very cynical, but I believe image plays the largest part in the establishment of most successful businesses. Look at the brand leader in any field of commerce you wish to choose, and then compare it, with the competition. In the vast majority of cases you will find that there is no appreciable difference between the product or service of the brand leader and the other half-dozen, or so, major companies in the field. What makes the brand leader stand out from the rest is IMAGE. Take, by way of example, McDonald's Hamburgers. McDonald's have such a strong image that they have pushed all other fast food shops into second place. Yes, they do have some good points where they genuinely score over the competition, but their success is due to their bright, spanking clean, 'switched on' image which is just right for the 1980's.

You may well be saying — "Image is all very well for consumer products, but it does not apply to me." Perhaps you are in electronics, with one or two large industrial contracts. "I don't need an image," you say. Yes, you do. Image is not just a question of having a snappy logo, and good packaging material. Image is all about having a clean, efficient office or workshop. Image is all about being the sort of person your customer enjoys meeting, talking to, relaxing with over a drink. Image starts with YOU.

Case study

About six years ago, my husband and a couple of colleagues, got together with the intention of starting a freight forwarding business. They had considerable experience in the industry, and gathered together a small team of people who they had worked with over the years and who were willing to join them in the new venture. Being a freight forwarder involved in air cargo meant they had to be based at Heathrow. They found premises, formed a limited company, borrowed some money and started trading as Overall Transport — international freight forwarders. What did they have to offer over and above their competitors? On the face of it, absolutely nothing. In the few square miles immediately around Heathrow, there are no less than two hundred and fifty freight forwarders — most of them well-established companies. Overall Transport needed an image which would project them into the market-place. For some days they agonized over the problem. There was no question of undercutting the rest of the competition. As we have already discussed, this is no method for breaking into a new market, it just causes a price war. Their premises were no better, and a good deal smaller than most, their transport facilities adequate, but not special. What did they have? The answer was simple — PEOPLE. Overall Transport can boast that it is a group of highly skilled, experienced people, with a thorough long-term knowledge of the trade. The image they have built is all about experience, integrity and personal service. So they projected the company on that basis, and today it is highly profitable, with branches up and down the country.

So how do you go about establishing a business image? Take a long look at yourself, and your business. What features are worth highlighting; what features does your business have which perhaps your competitors do not; what features do you think your customers would like you to have? Make a list of possible attributes and then carefully consider each one. You are looking for something that will stand the test of time. It is no good saying you are the cheapest, if you are not sure you can remain so.

Once you have decided how you are going to project your business, plug your image shamelessly, work it into your sales techniques, stress it in any leaflet or brochure you produce. If you can think up a short, snappy sentence, which sums up what you are trying to project, put it on your letterheading and business cards.

Case study

Some weeks ago I had a letter from a lady who is making lovely hand-knit chunky sweaters, with brightly coloured patterns and embroidery — all the rage at the moment. She wanted advice as to how to present herself to a large store, in a professional manner, in the hopes of obtaining an order. She had been given a good introduction to the store in question, but she was terrified of going along and appearing too amateurish. What could she do? I desperately wanted to help her — the sweaters were gorgeous, correctly priced and she deserved an order. I knew what she meant though, she did not want to come across as a housewife with a hobby. She wanted her merchandise to look and feel professional.

I suggested to her that she should firstly think up a brand name for her sweaters. They were aimed mainly at the late teens/early twenties, so I suggested she should think up something snappy and fun. Having selected a name, I suggested that she had a good quality label printed, and that she sewed the label into the neck of every sweater she was taking with her as a sample. She rang me up a few weeks later, absolutely ecstastic. She had just sewn in the labels and she said it made all the difference in the world. Instead of the sweaters looking like the product of a cottage industry, they suddenly looked professional.

She got her order, due far more to the excellence of her sweaters, than my label suggestion . . . but I think it helped!

Establishing an image does not mean spending money. Never take advertising space in order to promote your image. One frequently sees firms doing this, particularly in their trade press — it is an absolutely crazy waste of money. Only take advertising space if you want to sell something, buy something, hire someone, acquire new premises or whatever. From time to time as well as advertising, you will want to print letterheading, sales literature, carrier bags or packaging material. These are the vehicles which should carry your image, consistently and well. It costs no more to think it out carefully, and it could make a great deal of difference to the development of your business.

8. Can You Get At Them?

The need to study the accessibility of your customer.

I SEE NO CUSTOMERS

By the time you reach this chapter, your marketing plan should be pretty much complete. You know who, where and why your customer is; you know how your business compares with your competitors; you have decided whether it has a long term future; you have settled on the right price to offer, the right back-up services, and the way in which you are going to project both yourself and your business.

We are now left with the final piece in the jigsaw. I hate to say it, but asking yourself the following question could involve you in yet another re-think:

HOW ACCESSIBLE IS YOUR CUSTOMER?

The next section of this book — Reaching the Market-place — is devoted to the ways in which you can reach your customer. If you like, it is *practical marketing* — at the moment we are simply theorizing. Before we get to that section, I would like you to think in general terms as to the difficulties you are likely to encounter in sorting 'the wheat from the chaff' — in finding that splendid fellow who wants your product or service. Again, examples help, I think.

There are a great many overweight children in this country, and as far as I know there is no company specialising in manufacturing clothes for them. There is a real market there, ready to be cornered — a genuine need, and many a desperate parent would be only too happy to pay a little extra in order to have clothes that really fit. So if you were setting up as a manufacturer of clothes for fat children, how would you go about marketing the garments? Again, as far as I know, there are no retail outlets which specialize in the overweight child, and certainly no existing mail order catalogue. I think it extremely unlikely that you would be able to persuade a shop to devote a special area for your merchandise. It is possible that such a scheme might be considered in Central London, but fairly unlikely.

"Not to worry," you say, "I'll start my own mail order business." But to whom do you send your catalogue? Organisations such as Weightwatchers might help you, and a heavy advertising programme could result in a steady build up of appropriate names. It would be fatal, however, to send out a blanket mailing to everyone with a child. Whilst there are a lot of overweight children in the country, most children are not. Your response rate would be so low, it would put you out of business.

Do you see what I am saying? The idea is a good one and there is a real need in the market-place, but it is a brave man who tries to reach that market. The clothes industry is a good example. Either you, yourself, or someone you know, is bound to be above averagely tall, short, fat, thin, with particularly large or particularly small feet. There are thousands and thousands of us who do not fit into a standard clothes size and we are all constantly moaning that no one cares about us. They would do. It is just that they cannot afford to. The cost involved in winkling us out, is too prohibitive.

You and I know that given that your business idea is basically sound, if you could put twenty salesmen on the road tomorrow and spend half a million pounds on advertising, you would be on your way to establishing a substantial business. But most of us starting out in business do not have that sort of money available, and even if we did, we would be worried about the risk element involved.

Take as another example my lady with her Nigerian restaurant. She has an accessibility problem. If she could afford to advertise on a regular basis, in the whole of Surrey, I am perfectly certain that she could build up a regular clientele who appreciated the menu. It is unlikely, however, in the early stages, she can afford that sort of outlay. She must rely on the people of Weybridge for patronage, and only when her business is well established and profitable dare she risk a big advertising budget.

Accessibility is obviously a major problem to those businesses who intend selling a specialist product or service. It can also be a problem if you are selling to the mass market. An integral part of your marketing plan is HOW you are going to reach your customer. If you are going to approach your customer direct, you need to very carefully evaluate the marketing costs involved. They could prove prohibitive. If you are going to sell your product or service via middle men (i.e. wholesalers, retailers or industrial distributors) you need to establish two things:

1. Do you have a big enough margin to sell through someone else? — if a wholesaler is to stock and sell your product, he will require 20% or 30% margin for himself, a retailer will require at least 50% or 60%.

2. Have you the sort of product a middle man would be prepared to sell? We are back to the difference between buyer and customer again. You have to make sure that the product you have to sell is something a middle man will handle. Whilst consumers would welcome with open arms everlasting light bulbs or ladderless tights, I do not think wholesalers and retailers would do so!

As I hope I have demonstrated in these first eight chapters, finding a market is simply a question of asking yourself a series of practical questions, and the last of these must be:

HOW DO I REACH MY CUSTOMER?

If you cannot find a way without a disproportionate financial outlay, then sorry, you must scrub your whole business idea . . . and start again.

9. Are You Still Concentrating?

Monitoring — an integral and continuing part of the Selling Effort.

The successful acquisition of a place in the market is much like getting married — it is not the end, it is just the beginning. Just like marriage, the relationship with your market needs constant attention. Just like marriage, it can be very unpredictable at times, and needs to be worked at!

Monitoring means keeping a watching brief on your market, and frankly, this is vital. You need to be alert, and constantly on the lookout for signs of change and development. Can you provide, not only what your customer wants today, but what he is likely to want tomorrow? What is happening to the market in terms of technology, image and price? What are your competitors doing — can you keep pace with them and do you need to?

Before the world was hit by inflation, fluctuating money markets and microchips, business was a great deal simpler. I remember a conversation I had with my Grandfather some years ago, when we first suffered from inflation. He told me he had worked out that the price of his favourite brand of matches had remained static for the previous twenty-nine years. Yes, monitoring was not so necessary in the 1930's — in the 1980's, you will not survive without it.

You cannot look at your business in isolation — its development can, and usually will, be tremendously influenced by outside factors.

Here is a check list of those areas you should watch, constantly:

Trade magazines — if you are going to run your own business, from now on they should be your bedtime reading . . . sorry!

Competitors — send for all their sales literature on a continuing basis — call in and see them regularly (or get someone else to do so for you) — watch their prices — watch out for new products — listen to rumours in the Trade, particularly if they are in trouble — Perhaps, for example, they have let down one of their major customers. Move fast, you might be able to grab the business.

Local Affairs — where applicable, keep abreast with local developments, and above all local people — your bank manager, solicitor, accountant, Rotary Club, and publican are all useful sources of information.

Suppliers and their Representatives — suppliers should not be looked at purely as suppliers of goods, they are also suppliers of information. Representatives on the whole are terribly indiscreet. They will tell you whatever you want to know about your competitor — you only have to ask!

Consumer Information — if your product is ultimately being sold to the consumer, but you are selling via a wholesaler, do keep checking retail outlets. Selling through a wholesaler can alienate you somewhat from the market-place. You need to know what everyone else is doing.

I am not suggesting that your business should be subject to constant change. If you have found a good niche in the market, which is making you money, hang on to it. It is very precious. What I am asking you to do, is to be aware of potential dangers, and not be too complacent about your achievements. Also, it is worth considering that even if your product or service does not need any radical change, you might not be too wise to admit it. People are so easily impressed when commodities are dubbed 'the newest' or 'the latest'.

Case study

A few years ago, my husband bought a sewing machine manufacturing company. The company were specialists and had been trading for over fifty years. They were profitable, but sales had dropped off slightly in recent years. Immediately, the new management undertook a programme of market research, and after a few months, came to the conclusion that the machine being produced was exactly right for the requirements of the market at the time. The machine they were making was maroon, so instead, they painted it black, and re-launched it as 'This Year's Model'. Sales doubled.

Monitoring should not be looked at purely as a method of 'firefighting'. Carefully evaluating your market can also provide brand new business opportunities.

Case study

We have a friend called Jean, who is a portrait painter. For some years she has been accepting commissions for painting people — everything from portraits of children to great formal portraits of business tycoons, for the boardroom wall. She has found her life-style extremely nerve-wracking — always wondering where the next commission is coming from, and constantly worried about paying the mortgage. One day she painted the portrait of a little girl, together with her puppy. It was a charming composition. The delighted parents commented to Jean, at the time, that they were particularly impressed at the way she had captured the puppy. Jean has always thought of herself as a portrait painter, not as a painter of animals, but encouraged by the praise, she added to her little brochure that she would be pleased to accept commissions for painting family pets as well.

Her success has been amazing. From that moment she did not look back — commissions poured in. Thinking about it, it is understandable. There are quite a number of portrait painters about, but very few who specialize in animals. Also, with modern cameras, it is relatively easy to capture superb pictures of children, because up to a point, you can expect some degree of co-operation! Not so with animals. It is very difficult to persuade them to sit still in the right light for long enough. Jean saw a new market opportunity and reacted accordingly. She does not worry about her mortgage these days.

Monitoring should always involve a careful analysis of HOW you do things. Supposing you are a craftsman, who has built a business by making pine Welsh dressers, which you sell via a wholesaler. Because you are selling in this way, your profits are small, and you feel you are running faster and faster, just to stand still. The wholesaler will take as many Welsh dressers as you can supply him, but the more you make, the more staff you need, the bigger premises you require, and the profit margin just does not give you enough leeway to make a comfortable living.

What the wholesaler has done for you, as well as sell your merchandise, is to prove that there is a market for what you produce. It might be sensible to re-think your entire operation. Would it be better to have your own shop, or sell direct to the retail trade? You know the market is out there now. If you can reach it yourself, you are going to keep a great deal more of the profit.

Never lose sight of the fact that business today is extremely volatile. Your apparently safe market may have doubled, halved or completely disappeared by this time next year. So like the boy scouts, BE PREPARED . . . it is called MONITORING!

Section 2:   Channels

Having identified your market, the next stage is to find a way of reaching it. This is vital. There are so many different avenues of approach open to you, and choosing the right road can make all the difference between success and failure. The distribution process effects so many elements of your business — the price you charge, the type of presentation, method of manufacture, business image — all these factors, and many more, will be greatly influenced by whether you are selling direct to the consumer, or via a wholesaler, through an industrial distributor, or by setting up your own retail outlet.

This section will explore the various methods of reaching your market-place, and is sub-divided as follows:

Channels of Distribution for your Goods

Chapters 10 to 14 deal with the selling of a product, whether you are a manufacturer, or indeed, are part of the distribution chain yourself — i.e. a shopkeeper.

Channels of Access for your Service

Chapter 15, deals with the way in which you reach your market if you are selling a service.

Whether it is a product or a service you are selling, I cannot stress enough how important it is to find the right approach to your customer. Establishing a market is important, employing the right selling technique is important, but unless you use the right channel through which to reach your customer, your selling and marketing skills will be of little use.

10. Channels of Distribution – For Your *Product*.

The various options.

You have a product — you have a market, now you have to find a way of introducing the former to the latter.

The following diagram illustrates the possible links in the chain for the distribution of your product.

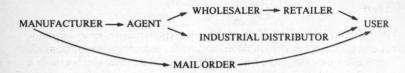

This diagram is not intended to infer that all these links are necessary — they are simply possible options. For example, a manufacturer can deal direct with a user. The most obvious example of this is mail order, but it could equally well be a craftsman selling his merchandise to the general public, direct from his workshop. You can also jump on and off the chain at any point. You might be setting up your own wholesale warehouse and then selling direct to the user, cutting out the retailer completely.

The further removed from the user you are, the bigger profit margin you will need. Middle men cost. Let us look at the diagram again, this time showing the gross profit/commission which will be required by each of them:

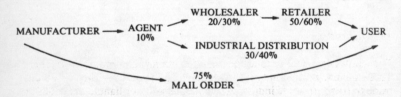

On face value, it would appear sensible to cut out as many links in the chain as you can, and, wherever possible, deal direct with the user. This is not so, for the following reasons:

1. The cost of dealing through middle men may seem high, but it can pale into insignificance compared with the cost of setting up your own marketing and selling operation.

2. Middle men are professional salesmen. On the whole, they are good at their job — working on commission, they have to be. They have the contacts and they have the knowledge of the trade. In many instances, it is far better to deal through them and accept a lower margin.

In the following chapters we will be discussing in detail, these various links in the chain and what they can do for you. Here is a brief resume of the functions of these middle men.

Agents

Having an agent is much like having a sales representative, except that it is cheaper. An agent is self-employed and works purely on commission. He supplies his own car, his own office and telephone, and specializes in a particular field of industry. He normally represents several businesses, selling their merchandise to his various contacts. It is these contacts that you are really buying when you appoint an agent. Most agents work on a 10% commission — i.e. that is 10% of your selling price, exclusive of VAT.

Factors

Factors are much like agents, with one notable difference. Factors actually buy your merchandise and then sell it on to their contacts. Again, the commission they take is approximately 10%. Factors are not normally found in any form of consumer goods. They are usually to be found in traditional industries — engineering and its like.

Wholesalers

The wholesaler usually stands between the manufacturer and the retailer. There are many different types of wholesaling operation — they vary from trade to trade. In some industries, wholesalers do not handle the goods at all — the transactions are all on paper and they simply arrange for the manufacturer's goods to be delivered direct to the retailer.

In other industries, quite the reverse is true. We are all familiar with builders' merchants. This is a wholesaling operation. In this case, the wholesaler acts as a sort of collating house for the building trade. He opens a warehouse and gathers together, under its roof, all the different component parts which are required in the building trade. It is then a simple matter for the builder to come to one single point, from which to collect his requirements, rather than have to visit a dozen different suppliers. This type of wholesale operation is to be found in many different industries, electrical and haberdashery, to name just two, and essentially these warehouses can supply everyone, regardless of category.

Going back to the builders' merchant, they will deal with builders, they will deal with small retail outlets, wanting to buy in goods for sale in their shops, and they will deal with the general public. Wholesalers usually require a gross profit of between 20% and 30% on selling price, excluding VAT.

Industrial Distributors

The difference between industrial distributors and wholesalers is that with industrial distributors, there is no retailer involved. Like factors, industrial distributors tend to be found more often in heavy industry, as their name suggests. The user, in this case, is never the consumer. An industrial distributor will be the go-between for a manufacturer, who is making some component part for industry, and the user who is likely to be simply the next stage of the manufacturing process. Industrial distributors on the whole look for a slightly larger gross profit than the wholesaler − between 30% and 40%.

Retailing

Retailing is the shop operation. You could be dealing with a massive chain of departmental stores, or the local corner shop − both are retailers and so is a market stall! Anywhere that goods are put on display for sale to the general public is a retailing operation. Retailers normally require a minimum gross profit of between 50% and 60%, excluding VAT. In some high streets in major towns and cities, where rates and rents are very high, they need considerably more than that.

You see the problem you are up against? In order to sell your merchandise, you have to find the right mix of price versus the right method of distribution. It may be that you simply cannot operate through a wholesaler, because you do not have the necessary profit margin to do so. Alternatively, you may have the profit margin, but the goods you are producing simply are not the sort of thing a wholesaler will handle, and you are forced to go direct to the retailer.

I think it is time to stop sitting on the fence, quoting options, and instead, offer you a piece of advice.

As a general rule, in order to break into a market which is new to you, you need help − professional help. If you are handling, or indeed manufacturing, a specialist item, with appeal to relatively few outlets, and with a high order value (minimum £1,000), then it is just possible that you would be best advised to go direct to a retailer. If, however, you are manufacturing, or handling, a low cost item, with appeal to the mass market, operate through a wholesaler and possibly even an agent, as well. No small business today, selling a low cost item, can afford to mount its own selling operation. The only exception to this rule applies if your business is extremely small and parochial. In other words, if you are making ceramic mugs, you may have an outlet through your local china and glass shop. If you are not looking beyond that one shop as your sales outlet, that is fine. However, if you are ambitious and wish to produce mugs for a couple of dozen shops, then in my view, you should be looking for a wholesaler. You can afford neither the time, nor the money, to service this number of outlets.

If you believe you can manage without any middle men, do bear in mind that the costs involved in selling direct to the user can be enormous. See chapters on retailing and mail order.

How you distribute your goods can have such a vital effect on your business. I was talking to a colleague of mine the other evening about this subject and he told me a story. Apparently some years ago, he financed a man who was one of the pioneers in oil-fired boilers for domestic use. The company prospered, but its growth and development were slow. The boilers were sold either through builders or direct to the general public. One of the top salesmen within the company became disillusioned with the way the company was being run. He thought it a marvellous product, but considered it was being sold in completely the wrong way. He left, developed his own boiler and started his own company. He sold his boilers entirely through wholesalers. Within a matter of a few months, he had nation-wide coverage and by the end of his first year of operation, he had overtaken several times the sales of his former employer. That company is now a household name and it owes its success to its distribution policy.

In the following chapters we will find the right method of distribution for your business.

11. Agents.

Selling to one — being one.

Good agents are very useful people — a great boon to industry as a whole. When one thinks of agents, it is more often in the context of their representing freelance services — i.e. actors, writers, etc. However agents are also very active in the distribution of goods, and it is in this role that we will consider them in this chapter. (*Note* — what follows, equally applies to factors, as well as agents.)

Selling through an agent

Finding an agent at all is quite difficult — finding a good one, still more so. Open most trade papers and you will see a great many advertisements seeking agents — usually far more than the rest of the classified advertising put together. I mention this not to depress you, but to emphasize that once you have found a good agent, look after him.

What are the advantages of employing an agent? Small businesses, particularly if they are new, are taking a terrible risk in employing a sales force. Even if your salesmen are employed on a commission only basis, there is still the question of a car, expenses and the sheer administration involved in controlling them. Agents work freelance. They meet all their own expenses, operate their own schedule, provide their own transport and are looking purely for a commision, usually 10% of the selling price, excluding VAT. It is because of this fact that in the early days you may have a problem actually finding an agent to represent you. All an agent has to sell is his time and it is vital, from his point of view, that he uses his time effectively. He has to be convinced that representing your product is going to be worthwhile for him, as well as for you. If he is good, he will have a range of valuable contacts and this is really what he is selling — his ability to 'get you in' to a customer who, otherwise, would prove inaccessible.

Good agents have contacts. They should also have the ability to provide a tip-top selling service. Efficient agents will travel the length and breadth of the country, if necessary, to see that samples are delivered on time. If they are clever in their presentation to potential customers, they will manage to convince the buyer that they are working for him, as well as you. Agents rarely work for one company — they work for several within an industry. This gives them a unique feel as to what is going on in their particular trade, and this they should be able to convey to the buyer.

Case study

By way of example, I was in the footwear buyer's office of a major mail order company some weeks ago, where an agent was finalizing an order. Having agreed the price, the buyer said that he would like to place an order for six dozen pairs of shoes, in each size, in each colour. The agent threw up his hands in horror and said that the manufacturer he represented could not possibly produce such a small quantity. It was not worth setting up the machinery to do so. The buyer countered by saying — "Either you accept the order as it is, or else I will have to look elsewhere."

The agent, being an agent, rather than a salesman representing one company, was able to say with authority — "The problem is, knowing the trade, as I do, you won't find any manufacturer who will make up such a small quantity of shoes for you".

It may have been just a good story, or what he said may have been true. Either way, the buyer believed him and so did I. He got his order for twelve dozen pairs of shoes in each size, and each colour!

If you acquire an agent, (or series of agents), to help you develop your sales, look after him. Make sure he has plenty of samples and point of sale material. When he rings up asking for a sample order, drop everything and make sure he receives it on time. The day he cannot rely on you to back up his selling effort, he will drop you, and quite right too. Selling is a tense business and if he is on to a red hot lead which he needs to follow up immediately, you must react accordingly. It could be panic samples, or he may require your presence in Liverpool in three hours flat. Whatever it is, do as he asks. If you fail to do so, not only are you wasting his time, you are wasting your own in hiring his services.

For the first time small business, I cannot recommend agents too highly. In fact I would go so far as to say, that as part of your market research programme, you should actually go through the exercise of seeing whether you can persuade an agent to represent you — assuming, of course, it is relevant to your particular industry. An experiment such as this will give you a very good idea as to whether your product is worthwhile.

Finally, how do you find an agent? Your trade papers are the best bet, or, alternatively, nick one from a competitor!

Being an agent

Being an agent is quite a good way to start your own business, *provided you have the contacts*. I would stress this question of contacts, since, quite frankly, if you have no known market to approach, there is absolutely no point in your setting up as an agent. You cannot afford to break totally new ground when you are having to meet your own expenses. Having said that, the contacts you have in industry might be approached, very effectively, in a completely new way. Let me give you an example.

Case study

In our first book in this series *Starting a Small Business*, we mentioned, as a case history, a knitwear agent called John. John and his wife run an extremely successful agency. They have only been in business for about six years and they drive a spanking new Rolls Bentley! For most of his working life, John has been a printer, and as such, has worked regularly with many of the major mail order companies. Over the years he made a great many friends, and has been involved quite often with the buyers when it comes to approving the colour reproduction of his catalogue opposite the garments themselves. In his early forties, he was made redundant with little immediate prospect of a new job. By sheer chance he was living in Leicester, the heart of Britain's knitwear industry. As part of his apprenticeship some years before, he had worked with knitting machines and therefore had a good working knowledge of how knitwear was put together. With his contacts in mail order and several hundred knitwear manufacturers on his doorstep, suddenly he had a business opportunity, and a very successful agent he has become. If you are considering being an agent, therefore, do not waste time wondering WHAT you know. Concentrate solely on WHO you know and whether there is anything you can sell them!

In the previous section of this chapter, we have discussed what makes a good agent and these lessons should obviously be applied to you, if you are contemplating becoming one. Whatever you do, keep your overheads at an absolute minimum. Although John drives a Rolls Bentley — we all have our idiosyncrasies — his office is still the kitchen table, his wife is still his secretary. To be an agent, all you need is a desk, a car, two telephone lines — one for incoming and one for outgoing calls — and an answering machine. Bear in mind, if a customer cannot reach you, he will simply ring someone else.

To be a successful agent, you need to be gregarious, outgoing, enthusiastic and prepared to drop everything when a customer calls. What you are offering is a service. A customer can perfectly well ring round a number of manufacturers to find what he wants. He uses an agent for convenience and you do need to be extremely efficient in all your dealings.

A note of caution. Once you are established, you should try to secure your position formally — i.e. you should try to obtain the odd contract to represent someone regionally, or nationally, over a period of time. In the early days, however, your agency arrangements may well be fairly informal and you do need to be careful. Once you have established a good working relationship between the manufacturer, or wholesaler, you represent, and the customer, there is a very real danger that they may cut you out. It happens all the time and in some instances, the manufacturers really cannot be blamed.

Case history

John told me quite recently of a case in point. For approximately two years, he supplied a major retail chain store from several different knitwear manufacturers. The store waited until John was on holiday and then approached each of the manufacturers in turn and said that they no longer wished to operate through John (they wanted to save the 10% commission). The manufacturers had a choice. Either they could deal direct with the chain store, or not at all. British knitwear is fairly hard hit at the moment and these small manufacturers could not be blamed for accepting the former. The interesting thing is that several months later, John tells me that three out of the four manufacturers involved have lost their contracts with the chain store and have come back to him for help. The reason for this, he believes, is that, as manufacturers, they were not able to supply the service the store required. For example, the customer may well ring the Managing Director of a knitwear manufacturer on Wednesday and say he wants to see the Spring range on Thursday at his office, a hundred miles away. The chances of a Managing Director being able to drop everything are slim. He has a factory to run. If the chain store had rung John, he would have been there.

So be on your guard for this problem. The golden rule for being a successful agent is not only to be indispensible, but to make absolutely sure that everyone knows you are!

12. Wholesalers and Industrial Distributors.

Selling to one — being one.

The difference between a wholesaler and an industrial distributor is this — the wholesaler sells to a retailer who, in turn, sells to the user. An industrial distributor sells direct to the user. Some trades use wholesalers, some industrial distributors, but as the name suggests, industrial distributors act as selling agents for industry — i.e. they buy from industry and sell to industry, such things as car components. Industrial distributors are never involved with consumer products. These are handled by wholesalers.

For simplicity's sake, in this chapter I am going to refer purely to wholesalers by name, but what applies to wholesalers, applies to industrial distributors.

In trying to assess whether you should be selling your product direct to your customer, or via someone else, you firstly need to decide what sort of business you want to be in. Supposing, by way of example, you are making pottery. If you enjoy making pottery, then essentially you are by nature a manufacturer. Once demand for your pottery comes from further afield than you local china shop, you are faced with a decision. Either you are going to continue to handle the manufacturing and find someone else to help you sell, or you will have to go out on the road and employ someone else to manufacture. The 'someone else to help you sell' could be a wholesaler.

Case study

A good example of how a business can completely change its original function is my own. Nearly ten years ago, I started a business manufacturing children's clothes. I felt there was a gap in the market for what I had to offer. Children's clothes have a tendency to fall into two categories. They are either cheap — well made, but in synthetic fabrics and rather basic colours — or they are very expensive — in good fabrics and good colours, but outside most people's budget. My aim was to provide good fabrics and colours at a cheap price.

I began manufacturing by using out-workers. I was very aware, being a mother myself, that there were many women with small children at home, who would welcome the opportunity of earning extra money. Within a matter of a few months, I had a good production team working in their own homes, and half a dozen seamstresses in a tiny workshop on my premises. Because my designs were different, I found a tremendous resistance among buyers in chain stores, and so after much soul searching, I decided to market the range myself, selling through mail order. By the time the business was bought by Damart eight years later, I had a very impressive turnover, which was many times beyond the capacity of my little team of seamstresses. Quite early on in the company's development I had to disband my team, and put the work out to factories large enough to cope with the demand. So what had happened? I had ceased to be a manufacturer and instead had become a marketing company.

This story, on the face of it, has nothing to do with wholesaling, but it does illustrate how you can start off as one type of business and end up as another. If it is your intention to be a manufacturer, then the employment of a wholesaler can help you to stay that way.

Let us look at the pros and cons of selling through a wholesaler.

Pros

1. *Preparing a costing exercise on launching a sales force is a very harrowing experience.* If you are looking to employ a salesman, with experience of your trade, and plenty of contacts; if you are going to provide that salesman with a car, a basic salary, a

commission and an expenses float, you are looking at spending £15,000 to £20,000 per year. There are many small businesses who cannot commit themselves to this sort of outlay, particularly when, however carefully you select your salesmen, the proof of the pudding can only be in the eating. Whether you are selling direct to a retailer, or indeed, the end user, it is a very expensive business. Unless you can be very sure of your success in selling direct, I should avoid it.

2. *Time* is also an important factor. Can you (and your staff) afford the time it will take to approach the market direct.

3. *Wholesalers are professionals* – they have the contacts, they know the outlets. If you do not have good personal contacts in the trade, then you should operate through somebody who does.

4. *Quantity and range of merchandise.* You should receive considerably larger orders from a wholesaler than from the average retailer. Wholesalers are less interested in a choice of goods. A visit to a retailer may well excite the reaction that they will try half a dozen of one type and half a dozen of another, three in one colour, three in a second. You can end up with a very 'bitty' order which is very difficult to manufacture. A wholesaler is more likely to find a market for one or two lines, and once these lines are established, he should place fairly large orders.

5. *Stability.* On the whole, dealing with a wholesaler gives a manufacturer a greater degree of stability and continuity. A retailer is much more likely to chop and change his requirements. He is the spearhead of the marketing operation, and therefore the most volatile and sensitive to change. Although on the one hand, this means that the retailer can take advantage of market trends, he can also make life very difficult for the manufacturer.

Cons

1. *Money is obviously the main problem.* It usually is! In order to sell to a wholesaler, you will need a very high margin in order to be able to provide enough gross profit, both for a wholesaler and a retailer. Your goods will have to be competitive.

2. *Volume.* Whilst you are in business to handle as many orders as possible, it is no good being swamped to the point where you cannot cope. Wholesalers require volume and the costs involved in providing sufficient facilities and machinery to cope with their demands, may prove prohibitive. You may find yourself in a position where you are making huge quantities of merchandise for a very small profit. The moment your operation starts getting big,

you will incur all the headaches such as large financial commitments, staff problems, etc., etc. Big is not necessarily beautiful.

3. *This tendency amongst wholesalers to 'think big' is a problem for the new business*. Whilst a retailer will be inclined to say that he would be happy to try a small quantity as a test, a wholesaler is far less flexible. Because he does not deal in small quantities, he is far less likely to try 'something new'. Whereas a retailer will be inclined to give a whirl to a new idea, a wholesaler will resist.

Names of appropriate wholesalers can be found either in your trade press or local yellow pages. How you approach them is important. You do need to make sure that you have all your facts at your fingertips, since a wholesaler will be as interested in your back-up services, as he is in the product itself. If the product you are selling is something which needs to meet official standards of any sort — such as health and safety — make sure you have this information available. Make sure, too, that you have at your fingertips such information as your production capacity, delivery time, discount structure for bulk orders and settlement terms. Be prepared to talk frankly about the financial implications of a large order. If a wholesaler is prepared to sell your merchandise, it is far better to be frank with him. Tell him right at the beginning of any shortcomings you may have, because of, say, your size of operation. Do not run the risk of letting him down. Be very aware of pricing structure. Not only yours, but his, and indeed the retailers. As already mentioned, a wholesaler will be looking for between 20% and 30% profit, and a retailer between 50% and 60%. You need to be convinced in your own mind that your product is good enough to stand this sort of margin.

If your product is in any way unique, you may find that a wholesaler asks for a sole agency, either for a particular area of the country, or, indeed, for the country as a whole. Be wary of this until you see how the wholesaler performs for you. The time to talk about a sole agency is when he has landed you a number of fine orders. Do not commit yourself too early.

If you are selling nuts and bolts, you will probably find it comparatively easy to find a wholesaler who will buy your merchandise, provided, of course, that it is up to standard on price and quality. Low cost items of everyday use, in other words, are relatively easy to sell. Where you may have problems is with high cost items, particularly when it comes to persuading a wholesaler to hold stock.

Supposing, for example, you had invented a fantastic new light-weight drill — the perfect gift for a D.I.Y. man. The kind of response you will probably receive from a wholesaler, is that they would be unable to handle it for you unless you could provide some form of advertising to promote it. In other words, without the product having a known public image, retailers would be unlikely to stock it. This is a tremendous generalisation, but it is the kind of problem that can arise. If you should find yourself in a position where every wholesaler you approach responds in this way, I think there is only one thing you can do. You would then have to make an approach to an established household name — such as Black & Decker — and try and persuade them to manufacture your invention under licence — in which case, they would promote it and would be responsible for distribution.

Wholesaling is a mixed blessing. Many a good idea has remained just that because its devisor has found no way of persuading a wholesaler to take up the cause, and has no money, or resources, to market the idea himself.

The golden rule is this. If you have a product to sell, which you can produce in volume, which has a small selling value and mass market appeal, then you need a wholesaler. If, on the other hand, your product has specialist appeal and a high selling price, you might well do better to market it yourself.

Being a Wholesaler/Industrial Distributor.

Although there are a few wholesalers who operate on paper only (in other words, they never handle or stock merchandise themselves), the vast majority of wholesalers and industrial distributors do in fact buy, sell and stock goods. Therefore they need two things — a considerable amount of capital and a large warehousing space with distribution facilities.

By definition these requirements take the operation outside the parameters of this book. Wholesaling is not small business.

If you are thinking of starting a wholesaling business, you need considerable experience in your particular trade, particularly as regards the selling operation. Wholesaling is capital intensive, not only because of the stock involved, but also because of the necessary investment in the selling operation itself. You will either have to employ salesmen or produce a large glossy brochure to sell your wares, or, more likely, both. Holding the right stocks, and gauging the right moment to offload them, is a very complex business.

If you are considering becoming a wholesaler, I would suggest you dismiss the idea, unless you have worked for some time in a wholesaling operation, and understand its mechanics perfectly and have excellent trade contacts.

13. Retail Outlets.

Selling to one — being one.

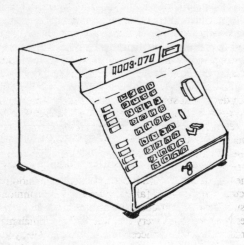

This chapter is divided into two sections — firstly, how to sell to a retailer, and secondly, how to be one.

Selling to the Retail Trade

There are basically three different types of retailing:

1. *The High Street shop* — which is likely to be part of a chain of stores. The position is first class, with a large passing trade, but rents and rates are high.
2. *The secondary position store* — very often described as 'a parade of shops'. These are usually independent, one-off outlets, selling a range of goods to the public in the immediate locality.
3. *That very British of institutions, the corner shop* — usually to be found in an otherwise completely residential area.

Whether you are the buyer for Marks & Spencer, or Mrs. Bloggs, from the post office stores, you do have one thing in common — your attitude to the merchandise, which is being offered. The primary concern of retail buyers is whether what they buy, then can re-sell at a good profit.

Before making your approach to any retail outlet, look first at what they are already selling. In the case of a big chain store, the goods on display will be the result of a careful computer analysis of those items most likely to attract a sale. In the case of the small shop, the merchandise very often reflects the individual taste of the shop's proprietor. So look, learn and listen all you can — there is no point in making an approach to a store where, quite clearly, your merchandise is unsuitable.

When dealing with the large chain store, you will find very often that the buyer knows precisely what he wants. It will then be a question of your deciding whether the product that you have to offer can be adapted in any way to meet his precise requirements, or whether it is unsuitable. In the case of the independent store, buyers are usually far more flexible. Many are tremendously influenced by trends and fashions. You will find it difficult to sell them a brand new concept, with no track record. Retailers are not pioneers. On the whole, they are far more likely to buy the type of merchandise which is already selling in shops similar to their own.

In the case of small retailers, consider very carefully the neighbourhood in which they are situated. You might have had tremendous success selling your particular product in a fairly up-market environment, but it might well be unsuitable in a poorer neighbourhood.

Big stores will also have a very clear idea of how much merchandise they wish to purchase. If you are successful in making a sale, you will receive an initial order and will be expected to undertake to back this up, within a very short space of time, if your goods sell well. In the case of the smaller shop, you need to be far more flexible. Do not be greedy. It is much better to accept a very small trial order to see how your goods sell, with the promise of repeat business, if all goes well. If a small shop places a large order with you, be warned. It means the buyer is a bad one, and if he is, it probably means the shop will go out of business and you might well lose your money.

With the larger chain store, all their promotional ideas will be handled by a central marketing department. In the case of the smaller shop, they might well welcome some advice from you on selling price, methods of display and an indication of your best selling lines.

So what are the pros and cons of trying to sell your goods direct to a retailer?

Pros

1. *Greater Profits*. If you are a manufacturer, going direct to the retailer obviously means that you will save paying commission to either an agent or a wholesaler. This means a high profit margin to you.
2. *Time*. Whether you are a manufacturer, a wholesaler, or an importer, there is a lot to be said for selling your merchandise through somebody else's retail outlet, rather than your own. Running a shop is very demanding, and if it is not your main business − i.e., for the sake of example, you are a manufacturer − it can take your 'eye off the ball' − in other words, it becomes more time-consuming than your main business function.
3. *There is a much larger range of retail outlets,* both in terms of size and type, than there are wholesalers. The bigger the choice you have, the more chance there is of finding a market.
4. *Flexibility*. Retail buyers are closer to the market-place, and therefore more susceptible to trends and new developments. Generally they are more flexible than wholesalers.

Cons

1. *Selling direct to the retail trade, can be a very expensive business*. Generally speaking, you should not attempt to sell direct to retailers if your product is aimed at the mass market and, most important of all, is a low cost item. If you are selling a specialist item of high value, you are far better selling direct to the retail trade, than through a wholesaler. The moment you start dealing in low cost items, however, the expenses involved far outweigh your potential profit margin.

   This, of course, does not apply if you are dealing on a purely local basis. If you are making ceramic mugs, you might well be selling them to two or three local craft shops − if you are making pâté, you might well be selling it to your local delicatessen and two or three pubs or restaurants. I am thinking of the slightly bigger operation, where you would be looking to sell to a dozen or so outlets − this is where it starts to become uneconomic.

   Alternatively, you might be able to find a way round the

problem of selling a low cost item. If, for example, you were manufacturing ceramic mugs, you could expand your range to include plates, teapots, jugs and bowls. Taking a large selection of products round with you might raise the level of your order value, which might, in turn, make the selling costs acceptable.

In general terms, however, if you are selling an item which costs less than a hundred pounds, you should either be looking at selling it on a purely local basis, or approaching the buying office of a chain store, which will involve one call, rather than many.

2. *The time factor.* Selling to the retail trade is not simply a question of popping in, delivering some goods and collecting a cheque. Retail outlets expect to be serviced as well. They want regular calls to check up on their stock position and deal with problems such as faulty goods. They will expect you to drop everything and react immediately if they have a run on any particular stock line. Even if you are selling durable goods, you may well find that an outlet requires two or three visits a month. Multiply that by six, say, and you could find that half your working life is spent servicing your customers. Can you afford the time?

3. *Bad Debts.* In the case of small shops, you do have to be very careful in the supply of merchandise. Many retail businesses hit financial troubles. Whilst it is very tempting to accept every order you can, be wary of the shopkeeper who insists on credit terms, from the moment you start trading. Take up references and only supply him with a very small quantity of merchandise until you have established if he is a good payer.

A friend of mine, a few years ago, started a business manufacturing leather belts. He decided to sell direct to the retail trade and in his first month of trading had tremendous success in off-loading his belts to a number of fairly classy boutiques. By the end of his third month, just over 50% of his sales had turned themselves into bad debts. Boutiques, of course, are notorious − they come and go − but my friend's leather belt experience is worth remembering. *A sale is not a sale until it has been paid for.*

4. *Retail Profits.* Except where food is concerned, you can be fairly certain that the very minimum a retailer will mark up the goods you sell him, is 100%. In some types of retail business, they will multiply their buying price by as much as 3. It is very tempting to speculate how much profit you could make if you could reach the customer direct − either by mail order, or through your own shop.

So in conclusion, if you can afford it, in terms of time and money, selling to the retailer can be a good idea. It means you keep more of your profit and it means that you are one step nearer your customer — always a good idea, as it helps you keep your finger on the pulse. Do be careful, however — you could so easily find yourself in a position where you are spending a great deal of time and money for very little reward.

Being a retailer

It is a fact that more small retailers go bankrupt than any other business category. Why is this? I think it is because running a shop appears to be an easy thing to do, whereas in fact it is difficult and fairly complex.

In the previous section, we discussed the three main categories of retail outlet. For the purposes of this chapter, I am assuming it is not your intention to open a large chain of shops. This being the case, forget the High Street — leave it to the 'big boys' — they have the capital resources, and the expertise, to maximise the sales and cover their overheads. High street rents and rates are astonishingly high — they are not for you.

This brings us to the secondary and tertiary positions, and I have to say right away that in many of these types of outlets, it is quite impossible to make a decent living. It is such a fine balancing act — if your site is a good one, the overheads will cripple you, if it is a poor site, you will not have enough trade. It is easy to find yourself in a 'chicken and egg' situation.

With any retail business, location is of paramount importance. Having established that the site is right for the merchandise you will be selling, you need also look at the competition. Too much competition obviously would be damaging, but no competition suggests that, perhaps, there is not a market for your goods in the area. One gets the impression talking to retailers, that very often they simply stumble into the retailing business because a shop becomes available in their area. Do not fall into this trap. Having decided the sort of merchandise you will be selling, and the type of people to whom it will apply, take time, plenty of time, to find the right location.

Retailing can be a very satisfactory business, but it is also extremely hazardous. I think it is worthwhile considering the following points before taking any steps towards acquiring a retail outlet:

1. Whilst it is possible to make a living, you are unlikely to become very rich from retailing. The surest way to make a success of a shop is to buy a premises which you can live above. This way, you can view the whole property as your home, and the shop operation itself is not crippled by high rent and rates.

2. I think you would be very unwise to acquire a retail business with a view to someone else running the shop. There are very few small shops which can be run profitably by anyone other than the

proprietor. In other words, to maximise your chances of success, buy a shop premises, live above it and work in it six days of the week, with the occasional half day off so that you can cope with the buying.

3. You need to recognize the time element involved in retailing. For most small shopkeepers, if they actually worked out what they earned per hour, they would find they would be far better employed in almost any other job however menial. Shop hours are long enough, but before you open there is the stock to be arranged, and after you have closed, there are the books to be kept up to date. Retailing is a job which needs physical stamina. If you are not prepared to work hard, very often twelve hours a day, then you should not go into retailing.

4. Do you like people? It is absolutely essential to enjoy meeting people. If you do not have a high regard for 'the Great British Public', you will make a hopeless shopkeeper! Liking people and wanting to please them is an integral part of successful retailing.

Once you have made your decision to go ahead and run a shop, there are four vital factors which stand between you and success, these are:

Stock
Presentation
Promotion
Competition

Stock

This is vital. The right stock in the right quantity is the only way you are going to make a success out of retailing. Avoid committing yourself to buying too much of anything, until you have established your customers' requirements. Keep your mind flexible and alert to possibilities, while at the same time avoiding too many risk items.

Presentation

Presentation is not simply a question of laying out your stock in an attractive way. You need to consider the practicalities as well. It is a fact, for example, that clothes sell better on a rail than on a shelf; that people do not like to stoop down, so merchandise on ground level sells poorly. These sort of factors are obvious if you think them out, and in planning your shop layout, you must make every item of merchandise as accessible and easy to see as possible.

Presentation is also about atmosphere.

Examine in your own mind why your favourite shops are your favourite. Yes, they sell the merchandise you require, but nine times out of ten, it is the friendly, cheerful atmosphere which brings you back, again and again. Your shop needs to be welcoming, without over-pressurizing your customer. It is vital to express an interest in your customer, whether they make a purchase or not. I am sure we have all had the experience where the moment the shopkeeper has taken your money, or indeed established that you are not going to make a purchase, he immediately looses interest in you. This is very bad retailing.

Promotion

Never be satisfied with the customers you have and the amount of merchandise you are selling. Find ways to maximise every possible opportunity for greater sales. Free publicity through your local newspaper's editorial department, can bring fresh customers. Door-to-door leaflet distribution and a small advertising budget can help, but only if it is offered in such a way as to really encourage people to come and see you. For example, if you are going to advertise in your local paper, design the advertisement with a coupon to clip. Invite readers to bring the coupon along to your shop, which will entitle them to a discount of 10%, or 50p, or £1, whichever is appropriate. This gives people some reason for coming to see you.

As well as bringing in fresh customers, look at ways of increasing the value of your sales. People cannot resist a bargain. Offer something free if they buy something else; offer a discount if sales are over a certain value. Do not be satisfied with selling £5 worth of goods to your customer − £6 would be better.

Competition

Use the competition to learn. If you are in the dress business, spend a day at Marks & Spencer watching what sort of merchandise they have on major display, and what items sell in terms of size and colour. If you run the corner shop, spend a day in your local supermarket doing the same thing. Particularly where provisions are concerned, it is easy to fall into a trap. You say to yourself, for example, that you have no call for grapefruit, but is that because you do not stock any grapefruit? Ask your customers what they want, how they view your shop in relation to your competitors. Retailing should be a continual learning process.

Remember retailing is not just restricted to the shop premises. Market Stalls are an excellent way to begin a retailing business − indeed several famous chain stores started this way. Your Local Authority will be able to advise you about rates for hiring a stall. There is usually quite a waiting list in the popular markets, though you may be able to persuade a friendly stallholder to sublet a piece of his stand. The items you sell from a market stall should be cheap and eye catching and you will certainly learn a great many valuable lessons from your fellow stallholders.

Another angle to the retail trade is the 'shop-within-a-shop'! You usually need to be a recognized brand in order to qualify for this type of trading. What happens? You rent a space in a large store — normally a department store. You display your merchandise under your own brand name, the store's staff usually sell for you and you give the store a percentage of your sales. The deals vary slightly but you do need an established product to attract a store to the concept.

Retailing is hard work, but it can be very rewarding. It is not the kind of business where you can ever say 'I've made it'. *Your business is only as good as the stock you have at the time, and your ability to sell it.*

14. Mail Order Businesses.

Selling to one — being one.

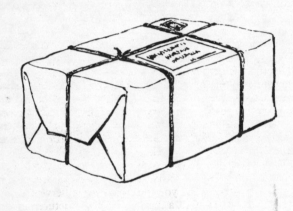

Mail order is a very specialist business, much more so than might be readily apparent. It can be a very good way of selling your product, but it is fraught with dangers.

Let us examine, first of all, the question of selling to a mail order house.

Selling to Mail Order

The areas on which most mail order catalogues concentrate are clothing, household goods, toys, and more recently, electronic games and machines. Mail order catalogues also extend to such merchandise as seeds, DIY equipment and teaching courses — such as 'Teaching Yourself to Write' or 'Speaking in Public'. However, it is in the field of clothing and small, light consumer products, where you will find the maximum choice of catalogues to approach.

Before making any approach to a mail order buyer, there are four golden rules which need to be applied to any product to ascertain its suitability for sale by mail order. These are as follows:

1. Is your product easily transportable, either by post, road or rail? This is not simply a question of weight, or even fragility. Modern packing is so clever that quite delicate items can be sent safely, and there is a great deal more flexibility so far as weight limits are concerned nowadays. No, you must also consider what your product will look like when it has been in a package for a week. Presentation is terribly important. Will your product appear tatty and crumpled, and if so, can something be done to improve presentation? Remember, in assessing your product for its mail order potential, do look at packaging as an integral part of what you have to offer. If the cost of postage and packing is too high, then selling by this method is non-viable.

2. Can you manufacture your product in a maximum of four weeks — in other words, can the process be undertaken from start to finish, including the acquisition of raw materials, within a four week period? This facility is absolutely essential for most mail order businesses. Buyers are simply not prepared to commit themselves to giving you space in their catalogue, if you are not able to provide back-up facilities.

3. For best results with mail order buyers, you need to offer a product with a little flair and originality. Buyers are shown the same thing over and over again, the same products appear in catalogue after catalogue Buyers are always on the lookout for something which appears new but is really the same. What do I mean by that? Mail order buyers are not looking for way out merchandise. Their business is built on selling classics, but what they like best is something classic with a new twist to it.

4. Your price needs to be extremely competitive. Traditionally the mail order trade is supposed to offer its customers goods at a price, which is less than they would expect to pay in the High Street. Nowadays this is not always true, particularly when you add in the postage and packing element. However, enough of this concept lingers to make it essential for mail order buyers to feel the prices they are offering are really competitive.

As a guide to selling price, if an item being sold is subject to VAT, the buyer will take your price and multiply it by three to find his selling price. If the item is zero-rated, he will multiply your price by 2½. On the face of it, these margins seem enormous, and to you, the manufacturer, trying to earn a living on something like a 30% gross margin, it probably appears scandalous. However, what you have to remember is that mail order buyers are providing all your marketing, and if your items prove to be a winner, you could find yourself being asked for orders of 30,000 or 40,000 units at a time. Two final points on the question of price — most mail order buyers, having fixed a price with you, then quote you discount terms. Unlike, I think, almost any other industry, mail order buyers usually expect a 6% discount for settlement in seven days. You do need to take account of this figure in your costings since it is unusually high. The second point is that mail order buyers are usually fairly 'red hot' — they do know their market. Not only do they see many representatives every day, they also work surprisingly closely with their competitors. There is a great deal of swapping of information between catalogues on the question of price, quality, popular colours, etc.

So, in assessing your product for its suitability to sell by mail order, carefully consider these four points. If it comes up to scratch, then here are a few hints on how to approach a mail order buyer.

You do not need to be a professional salesman to sell to mail order buyers. Surprisingly, considering the enormous sums of money they handle they are very accessible. Always ring and make an appointment, clearly stating what you have to offer, to ensure you see the right buyer. In a large company, for example, shoes may be handled by one buyer, but trainers will come under the heading of sportswear and be handled by another, so it is very important to make sure you are speaking to the right guy.

Mail order buyers do not have much time. As well as the endless stream of potential suppliers, they are also dealing with a very volatile trade. During the course of the day in which you see them, they will experience a number of crises. Mail order is such an unpredictable business — some obscure little dress that they have pushed into the bottom left-hand page, mid-way through the catalogue, could suddenly prove to be the winner. Suddenly they have to find 30,000 dresses in three weeks. The fabric is in Hong Kong and the manufacturer is on holiday. See what I mean? Therefore, prepare what you have to say to him carefully.

There is absolutely no point in taking along a product unless you have a price list. You must also have a very clear idea of your delivery performance and do not try to mislead him — he is probably too smart for that. For example, if you appeared on a buyer's doorstep with, let us say, a gingham shirt for sale, you might be tempted to say that you can guarantee a three week turn-round. A buyer worth his salt will feel your cloth and say "This cloth is imported. What guarantees have you got that you can meet any orders I place with you?" You need to be ready for that question. Perhaps you are prepared to hold back-up stocks of raw material, or perhaps your U.K. fabric supplier will do so. Mail order buyers are shrewd — do not underestimate them.

Buyers see a great deal of merchandise in the course of a week and because they are always moving from crisis to crisis, they tend to live in a total state of chaos. Whatever your product, make sure attached to it is a label clearly stating the price, your name and telephone number. After you have gone, your product will be thrown in a heap, or on a rail, with everyone else's. You must make sure it can be readily identified.

Remember too, that mail order companies work a long time ahead, and are very seasonal. Catalogues are usually produced twice a year — in January and July. Buyers are always looking nearly twelve months ahead, and normally their final selection of merchandise happens in March and August.

As already indicated, orders can be very large indeed. There is little point in approaching a major catalogue such as Littlewoods, Grattons, or Empire Stores, if your production capacity is very small. There are, however, a number of specialist mail order companies around who would actually welcome the opportunity of being able to place small orders.

If your product is selected for a catalogue, most companies will give you a small initial order, which is usually, as a rough guide, about a third of what they anticipate they will sell. Bear in mind, however, that such is the unpredictability of the consumer, that forecasts can be dreadfully wrong. The initial order is normally placed approximately three months before the catalogue is despatched to the public. Catalogues are rarely despatched all at once. The first batch sent out serves as a guide to the buyer, from which he will be able to gauge a total sales forecast. Therefore, once the catalogue has been out about three weeks if your product is selling well, you will receive a repeat order, together with an indication as to how much merchandise will be required overall.

Virtually all medium to large mail order companies use a computer these days. As well as speeding up the despatch and handling of orders, it also gives them access to a vast range of statistics. A good mail order company will be well aware of the most popular colours in a season, the most popular sizes, the most popular styles; what type of person is likely to buy your merchandise, at what time of year, and in many cases, even in what part of the country. When talking to a buyer for the first time, do not come across as being too much of a 'know-all'. He probably knows an awful lot more about your product than you do.

Selling by Mail Order

Many small businesses have tried to sell their merchandise by mail order
. . . and many have failed. The fundamental reason behind this failure rate
is over-optimism about the likely response to mailing shots and, or,
advertising.

Let us start at the beginning. Supposing you wish to market a range of
knitwear. You have looked at an approach to the retail trade and have
taken my point, from the last chapter, that it is unlikely to be cost effective
for you to trudge round a variety of small outlets. You do not feel your
products are right for a chain store operation and so you have decided to
go ahead and market the knitwear yourself. Mail order seems the obvious
answer.

Well it could be. But I would strongly recommend that if you have no
mail order experience, either you employ someone who has, or you work
for a big mail order company for a few months to learn how it is done.

There are two terms connected with selling by mail − mail order and
direct mail. Mail order is the term used for selling goods direct to the
customer through general press advertising. Direct mail means sending
direct to the home of potential customers, a brochure or sales leaflet
intended to generate a sale. Most mail order companies use both methods.

So how do you set up your own mail order business? I will pursue the
knitwear example. Apparently the easy way to start is to buy a list from
someone else, print a catalogue and despatch it to the people on this
bought-in list. There are a number of list brokers (your local advertising
agency should be able to supply you with a list of them) who charge
approximately £40 to £50 per thousand names. The broker supplies you
with a list of companies whose names they hold, the idea being, for
example, that if you wish to sell children's clothes, you would try to buy
the names of a mail order company who specialize in children's products.
This may seem the quick way to set up your mail order business, but I do
not rate it.

The problem is that someone else's names can well bring you in a
response rate of as little as 1% of the total mailing. Let us turn that into
cash terms. Supposing you sent out a ten thousand mailing shot.
Assuming you sent it second class and that your brochure, envelope and
order form cost you no more than 20p, you would be spending £4,000. If
you had a 1% response rate and your average order value was, say, £20
your total sales would be £2,000. You see what I mean? You would make
an absolutely thumping loss.

No, by far the best way to start a mail order business is to acquire your
own names. That can be done in two ways, either by press advertising, or
best of all, by a public relations campaign (see Chapters 18 and 19). It is a

much slower method, of course. If you persuade your local newspaper to run an article on your business, making sure they quote your address, so that people can write to you for a catalogue, you may find that you gather two or three hundred names. If you are lucky enough to persuade a national magazine or newspaper to write an editorial piece about you, you could receive several thousand. Either way, it is a lengthy process. It can be quickened up, of course by placing advertisements, but rather like buying a list, it is very easy for your expenditure to run away with you — more of that, later.

Let us look again at that ten thousand mailing shot. We will assume that you have built up ten thousand names by your own PR and advertising efforts. We assume that when these people have ordered from you, they have been well looked after, and that they are pleased both with the goods and the service. So again, you mail ten thousand catalogues and again it costs you £4,000. In these circumstances, however, your response rate should be approximately 7%, which at £20 an order would give you a revenue of £14,000. Suddenly you are in the mail order business!

So the message here is this. Do not start blindly mailing bought-in lists, or the telephone directory, or whatever. You must ensure the quality of every name to whom you send a catalogue. They must be people who want to buy by mail and they must be people who want to buy from YOU. At something like 35p a go you cannot afford to do anything else.

We have studied direct response, what about mail order? Press advertising is very expensive, and it is a very specialist business. Some publications, with an enormous circulation, and thus a very high advertising rate, generate a very poor response from direct mail advertising. If, for example, this knitwear you are producing is chunky countrywear, you would probably be far better taking advertising space in Farmers' Weekly than in a national newspaper. Advertising is discussed in depth in Chapter 18, but if you are considering spending more than £1,000 on mail order advertising, I would recommend that you employ the services of an advertising agency. Do not, however, choose *any* agency, choose an agency which specializes in mail order, since they will have a great deal of experience and should be able to advise you as to which media are the most likely to bear fruit.

This is a terribly sweeping statement, but as far as mail order is concerned, I think there are only two types of advertising which really work, and they could not be more different. One is a full page, in colour designed for maximum impact, with a coupon to clip from which readers can order goods direct. It is a tremendous risk but when it works, it is highly profitable. The other is a tiny black and white line drawing taking up no more space than a single column, by, say, ten centimetres, which you place in the same spot, week after week, in a newspaper or magazine.

For the first eight or nine weeks response will be negligible, but once people are used to seeing it there, if the advertisement is right, the response rate will start to grow.

As a general guide to mail order press advertising, you can expect a response rate of approximately 0.25% of the circulation of the publication.

Selling by mail order is not simply a question of placing the right advertisement, or designing the right catalogue. One of the biggest dangers is stock. Quite rightly, today, there is very stringent legislation to ensure that a company does not hold onto customers' money for more than four weeks, without either sending a refund, or the goods. This means that whatever you are manufacturing must have the facility of a very fast turnround. You must carry stock. Let us assume that you are going to offer twelve different styles of knitwear in your catalogue. Let us assume that this knitwear is being offered in three sizes, small, medium and large, and in three different colours. This means there are one hundred and eight different permutations — you have to stock one hundred and eight garments, just to have one in each size and colour. That is nearly £1,000 of stock before you start. Mail order will involve you in considerably more capital than you probably anticipate. *As a rough guide, when you are calculating how much money you will need, if you are anticipating a turnover in your first year of £50,000, then at any one time you will probably need to carry a stock at cost value of anything up to £10,000 to support it.* That stock has to be funded.

The other big financial commitment is with regard to acquiring a licence to advertise. If you are intending to advertise in a national newspaper and, *this is important,* are asking people to send you money, you have to have an NPA licence. (Newspaper Publishers' Association.) This is not easy, because currently, the NPA underwrite the cost to any readers, in any newspaper covered by their scheme, who lose their money — say because the mail order company goes bankrupt. The NPA will want reassurance as to your financial standing in the form of a bank guarantee and/or a Readers' account, into which readers' money is paid until they have received their goods. The former can be as high as £50,000, the latter can play havoc with cashflow.

Magazines have much the same scheme — only it is run by the PPA. Just a few regional newspapers and magazines are exempt from the scheme.

This obviously represents a major commitment on your part. NPA and PPA application forms can be obtained from your advertising agent or the advertising department of any publication in which you intend to advertise.

NB. Provided you are not asking for money, you do not need a licence.

In other words if you are simply asking people to send for your free brochure, no licence is required.

I mentioned in the earlier section of this chapter that mail order buyers multiply their buying price by three if the goods were subject to VAT, and by two and a half if they were not. You must do the same thing. Your marketing costs will be too high to do anything else. Similarly, in my view, it is out of the question to offer any item by mail order, which sells for less than £10. So far as direct response is concerned, you do need to be looking for a minimum order value of £20 to £25. If, in either case, the unit sales drop below this figure, you are going to be in trouble.

Most small mail order companies do not give credit terms, nor is it expected. You should ask for cash with order. This method of trading is very often misunderstood by people. It is assumed that because the business receives cash with order, they need no working capital, since this is provided by the customer. As I have just demonstrated, you will require a considerable cash outlay for stock. In addition, you need to bear in mind that sending out a catalogue is very much like playing roulette – you do have to gamble a considerable amount of money to see any return. Go back to our ten thousand mailing shot. We are investing £4,000, which will have to be paid for whether the response rate is 1% or 7%. Cash with order must not be considered as a method of funding your business. You need a good solid base of working capital before you start.

So the message for this chapter is this – whether you are selling to, or by, mail order, treat it with the respect it deserves!

15.   Channels of Access – For Your *Service*.

The various options.

The service industry is a very good one for the small businessman. Statistically, far more businesses who provide a service succeed, than those offering a product. Except for those businesses which require a specific location, most service industries need very little financial commitment. Many a highly successful business has been spawned from the kitchen table.

Very often offering a service is something that can be operated on a part-time basis, in conjunction with an existing job, only going full-time when pressure of work makes it necessary. Let us look at the various different categories of service industry:

1. *Professional Services.* For professional men, such as accountants or architects, there are plenty of opportunities to go freelance. This means that the professional man will work for a number of people on a part-time and/or temporary basis, selling his skills.

2. *Services to Industry.* At one end, this covers the consultants — self-styled experts in such things as computers and marketing. At the other end, there are the typing and secretarial agencies — in between a wealth of services to industry.

3. *Services to the Public.* This, as the title suggests, is where the service is directed at the general public rather than industry — window cleaners, plumbers, electricians, taxis, gardening contractors, builders, etc., etc.

4. *Retail Services.* This is where the service is again directed at the public, but requires a retail outlet in order to operate. Examples of this are, hairdressing, dry cleaning and travel agencies.

5. *Catering.* All aspects of catering could be described as a service industry, from take-away hamburgers to the most exclusive restaurant.

6. *The Arts.* Writing, painting, music, can all be provided in the form of a service.

Whatever your service, there is, without doubt, one common denominator. Generally speaking, from time to time, industry can supply the odd batch of shoddy goods and 'get away with it'. Not so with services. You can only build a successful business by providing quality, continuity and trust. With many services, what is being offered is intangible — *you have got to be good to be successful.*

Let us look again at the various categories of the service industry and see how each category can best find its channel of access to the customer or client:

1. *Professional Services.*

   Professional services are not something which can be channelled through an agent. This is the type of service business which is entirely dependent on knowing the right people. The tools of your trade are a good quality business card and the reputation for doing a first class job. Building a business in this particular sphere is likely to be achieved on a snowballing principle — word of mouth, personal recommendation, and gradually, a growing reputation.

2. *Services to Industry.*

   Services to industry require a more direct and aggressive approach to the client. Advertising in the Yellow Pages and recognised trade magazines is essential. If you are operating on a local scale, then delivery of a mailing shot to appropriate businesses is a good idea. A great many services to industry can benefit enormously by a close association with a business in a similar field.

Case study

I have some great friends who are public relations consultants. Two or three times a month they hold press conferences on behalf of clients, and, from my experience, they always use the same photographer to take the press shots. This is not because they are acting as his agent, or are taking a commission on his work. It is purely that he is good at what he does, charges the right rate for the job and is a pleasant and unobtrusive chap to have around. It is for this reason that they recommend him regularly to their clients. There are a great many informal relationships such as this which can be of enormous benefit.

3. *Services to the Public.*
   There can be no middle man involved here because, quite clearly, you are dealing direct with the consumer, and it is to them you should appeal. Again, however, close associations with other businesses, on an informal basis, are of enormous value. The taxi cab driver wants to make sure the local hotels and restaurants will ring HIM when one of their customers needs a cab. The electrician should aim to ensure that it is HE the local builder recommends for the installation of lighting for the new extension he is building.

4. *Retail Services.*
   The bulk of your trade walks past your door, and it is easy to become complacent. Do not be satisfied with what you have — look further afield. If, for example, you are operating a dry cleaning business, look to the local hotels, restaurants, hospitals, schools and general institutions for dry cleaning contracts. These contracts will pay the rent on cold, wet January days when you only have two customers in a whole afternoon.

   Also do not be wedded to the concept that you necessarily need a retail outlet, just because your type of service provides one.

Case study

Take hairdressing as an example. My mother used to visit a

hairdressers which closed down when the proprietor became pregnant. After the birth of her child, Anne, the hairdresser, began visiting individual homes and doing people's hair on the spot. The news spread and soon she had a large following. She found visiting an individual extremely profitable, but gradually one or two women clubbed together so that she could cut and wash several women's hair in one home. Two babies later, she now admits to my mother that she is making a great deal more money operating her hairdressing business like this, than she ever made with a large retail outlet and a number of staff. So whatever the service you are offering, do make sure that your overheads are kept at an absolute minimum, and do not be hidebound by the traditional way of running the service. There could be short cuts.

5. *Catering*.

The traditional restaurant, pub, hotel and fast food outlet operate as any retail trade — by direct access to the public. However, there are a number of ancillary services connected with catering, which are well worth exploring. On a small scale, specializing in home-made quiches, pâtés and puddings, may well be a service appreciated by your local restaurant or pub. On a larger scale, there is quite a degree of scope for providing freelance catering services for functions.

Case study

We have some friends who run an excellent country pub, who are now making a great deal of money from outside catering. Two housewives, with children off their hands, approached our friends Betty and James, a few years ago and suggested that if they provided the catering, Betty and James could provide the bar and licence for outside catering events. They began slowly, with a few weddings and private functions, moved to horse shows and company Christmas parties, on to large receptions, banquets and balls. If you have a flair for catering, it is well worth while trying to team up with someone who can provide bar facilities and a licence. There is big scope in that area.

6. *The Arts*.

Writers, artists and musicians fall into two categories — commercial and non-commercial. By way of example, journalists, graphic designers and the composers of advertising jingles, would fall into the category of being commercial artists. They work freelance, offering their wares to a variety of newspapers, magazines and advertising agencies. In the case of say, authors, portrait painters and composers, they normally employ an agent to sell their work. Agents are useful. As with selling a product, they have the contacts, the selling skill and are only paid on achievement.

As a general rule, the type of service you are offering tends to dictate the channel by which you reach your customer, or client. Do not, however, blindly follow the same route as everyone else. Be alert at all times, not only to the requirements of your customer, but also the possibility of who else will have ready access to him. If you are a freelance accountant, for example, it is imperative that every bank manager in your area is aware of the service you offer. If you are a computer consultant, it is imperative that every office equipment supplier in your area is aware of the service you offer.

In the service industry, it is the informal relationships between people and businesses, with a common interest, which are usually of the most value.

Section 3.   Selling

Selling is believing, selling is having enthusiasm and the ability to convey it, selling is all about having confidence in yourself and in your business.

This next section of the book is concerned with the tools you need, both to sell and to reinforce your selling effort. You may be going to employ an agent, a salesman or take on a partner to handle sales, but that does not mean you can ignore the selling skills. Salesmanship will obtain for you a bank overdraft, a lease on some premises, discount terms, sixty days' credit or editorial space in your local newspaper — the need to sell stretches far beyond the requirement to simply obtain orders.

There is no substitute for enthusiasm. Creating your own small business, in itself, can make a salesman of you. Whilst you may not be able to sell other people's merchandise, it is quite another story when it comes to selling your own.

For all that, some of the very best ideas have fallen by the wayside because there was no one to sell them — so let us make sure that yours is not one of these.

16. Have You Got What It Takes?

A review of selling techniques.

In the early days of most small businesses, the selling is very often undertaken by the principal. Whether his business idea sinks or swims, depends entirely on his ability to convey it to other people.

Even if you are not going to undertake the direct selling of your product or service yourself, the success, or otherwise, of your business will largely depend on your ability to persuade others to have faith in it.

Salesmen are made — they are not born. Selling is not some obscure skill with which a few are blessed. What is required is the ability to deal with people, combined with common sense and a little elementary psychology. In our day-to-day lives, we are all salesmen up to a point — convincing the wife that a trip to the pub is essential, convincing the baby that it really is happy sitting in its high chair, convincing the dog that chairs are for people and floors are for animals.

It is an old adage but a true one — when selling anything, *first* you have to sell yourself and *then* you have to sell the merchandise you have to offer.

Enough philosophizing — what do you actually have to do to make a successful sale? First of all, before approaching anyone, you need to sit down and do a lot of thinking — think about your product, think about your business and plan your sales approach.

Your Product

You believe in your product (or service) or you would not have built a business around it. However it is only realistic to recognize that most merchandise has drawbacks of varying sorts. You need to understand these and be prepared to counter any criticism, with a justifiable plus point. There is one thing worse than a buyer discovering the shortcomings of your product, it is the buyer discovering that you are unaware of the shortcomings of your product.

Your Business

Unless you have been established in business for some time, a buyer is likely to query its stability very early on in the meeting. You need to be ready for that one. It may be that you genuinely have a very strong financial base, in which case tell the buyer so. If, however, like most of us in the early days, you are struggling a little, you are going to have to look for other merits. It is quite wrong to mislead the buyer into believing you are much bigger and better established than you are — he will find out the truth and his subsequent lack of faith will almost certainly lose you future business. No, what are your assets? Most probably the main one is you, yourself. Perhaps you have had years of experience in the trade, or employ somebody else who has; perhaps you are aware of the buyer's need for a particularly personal service, which only a small company can provide; perhaps the size of your business means you have small overheads and therefore can offer extremely competitive terms. What you have to point out to a buyer is that he cannot 'have his cake and eat it' when dealing with a small company. You need to emphasise your many qualities and make sure they outweigh your possible vulnerability.

Your Sales Approach

A planned approach is terribly necessary. Here are some golden rules, which are worthy of consideration before presenting yourself to your potential customer:

1. *Trial Run.* If you have a new business and a new product, never make your first sales approach to the company, or individual, you think most likely to buy your merchandise. You need a few 'dummy runs' and a little experience before taking on 'the big one'. Good buyers can ask some awful questions – questions that never, in your wildest nightmares, would have occurred to you. You do need some experience of being able to handle these before approaching your most potentially valuable customer.

2. *I believe that as a general rule you should always make a telephone appointment first,* before calling on a buyer. This does not mean to say that if you happen to find yourself in an area, with time to spare, and spot a likely-looking firm, that there is any harm in calling in and seeing if the buyer is available. In these circumstances you might strike lucky, but usually it is best to make an appointment first. It is courteous to make an appointment – it is also practical. A great many buyers simply will not see a salesman without an appointment, and when running your own business, you cannot possibly afford to go tramping round the country making abortive calls.

3. *The telephone call.* Do not be trapped into talking too much when you ring up for an appointment. The very best approach, if you can manage it, is to find someone who has access to 'the Great Man's' diary and fix an appointment without even speaking to him. This way you will not be quizzed too much. If you do end up speaking to the buyer, do not be drawn into a long conversation as to what you have to offer. It is terribly difficult to be convincing over the telephone unless you have been trained in telephone sales. When faced with the question "Why do you want to see me?", say something along the lines – "Because I have a product in which I think you would be interested." If you are forced into giving further details, try and convey that you feel the buyer would be missing something important if he does not see you, and that it is far easier to explain what you have to offer by seeing him face-to-face. If he persists, you will just have to do the best you can with a selling job over the telephone.

4. *The Appointment.* Never see a buyer too early in the day, or too late in the afternoon. He is likely to be at his most receptive

mid-morning, with the post cleared away from his desk and his mind still fresh. The later in the day it becomes, the more jaundiced he is likely to be.

5. *Do not be depressed if your first visit does not result in an order* – frankly it is fairly unlikely to. What is terribly important at that first interview is to listen and learn. Take an intelligent interest in what your buyer has to say. What product is he using at the moment? How much? How often, and at what price? Learn as much as you can about his business and learn as much as you can about the man. Do not be too pushy. Be alert and interested.

6. *Buyers are busy men.* Whilst they need basic information concerning you, your business and your product, they do not need a personal autobiography. I must have seen hundreds of representatives over the years and the one thing that really drives me mad is the 'woolly' approach. This is the representative who seems willing to talk about anything – the weather, the state of the country, his children, your children – but the real reason for his visit. When eventually you do drag him reluctantly to discuss what he has to sell, he is ill-prepared. He will have to go back to the office and work out a price; he will have to look at his delivery schedule before committing himself on how long it will take to fulfil the order. If you cannot even be efficient in the presentation of the information your buyer is likely to require, he is unlikely to have much confidence in your ability to supply the goods.

7. *Closing a Sale.* It is terribly difficult to generalise on this technique. The best advice I can give you is to rely on instinct until you gain experience. Not very helpful, I am afraid, but knowing the right moment to strike is very similar to trying to land a salmon! If you apply pressure too soon for a decision, your buyer may turn you down flat – on the other hand, give him too much time to make up his mind and you may find someone else has beaten you to it. One of the most dangerous people around is the 'kind' buyer. Buyers are not all ogres and many of them are very attracted by the idea of giving a small business a helping hand. You may spend a great deal of time, on their behalf, producing samples to their specifications, dashing backwards and forwards with prices and taking them out to lunch. Yet, basically for one reason or another, what you have to offer may not come up to scratch. In these circumstances, the 'kind' buyer finds it difficult to tell you so, and he may prevaricate for weeks, saying he is waiting for a decision from

head office, or whatever. What he does not realise is that he is hurting you far more by not advising you of the true position, because whilst you still think he may give you an order, you are wasting precious time and energy on him. If you suspect you are falling victim to a 'kind' buyer, you are going to have to force a decision out of him.

8. At the point at which you are trying to close your sale, and you feel the order slipping away from you, you must quickly undertake a salvage operation. If the buyer starts to say something along the lines that basically he is happy with his current supplier, and he cannot really justify moving his business to a smaller organisation, particularly since he is worried about your ability to cope etc., etc., – you do have a defence. Suggest to him that you can well understand his reluctance to change suppliers, so how about giving you just a piece of the business, on a trial basis? If you can just get that one order, however small, you have your toe in the door. Once you have formed a supply relationship with your customer, then it is up to you to work hard and gradually aim to take a little more of the business as each month goes by. The existing supplier is likely to be complacent. If you can be particularly efficient and attentive, you stand a good chance of ending up with the total order.

9. *The follow-up technique.* I do not care how abortive your sales call may have been, every call you make must be followed up by some literature in the post, to arrive on the buyer's desk no later than thirty-six hours after your visit. Hopefully you may have been asked to send samples and a quotation. If it will take, say, a week or ten days for the samples to reach your buyer, do not allow that time to pass without communication, even though he knows the samples will take that long. Write to him immediately, thanking him for his time, giving him a quotation if he requires it, and confirming that the samples will be despatched to him within ten days, or whatever. At the other end of the scale, if the buyer says he has no interest in what you have to offer, still write. Again, thank him for his time, enclose whatever sales literature you have, and ask him to bear you in mind should circumstances change. The object of this communication is three-fold:

a) A fast follow-up procedure will impress the buyer. It will confirm that you are efficient and, as we have just said, if you are efficient at selling, it suggests you are efficient at supplying whatever it is you have to offer.

b) Secondly, this approach puts you one ahead of the 'woolly' salesman. What every buyer wants is a simple piece of paper giving him all the information he requires on your product or service. Whether it is of any use to him currently, or not, if he has all the information he requires nicely documented, it will go in a file rather than the waste paper basket.

c) Lastly, your letter will remind him of your visit and YOU, and will tend to fix the memory of you and your business in his mind for the future.

10. *Record Keeping*. It is essential that you keep a card index on all your potential customers. The moment you come out of your meeting, sit down and write up your card. Obviously, there will be important pieces of information – the buyer may have asked you to ring in three weeks time, or supply samples, or quotations. There are also the less obvious pieces of information which may well be useful in the the future – the name of his wife, his secretary, how many children he has, etc., etc. Indeed, any details connected with the buyer, or his company, should be jotted down. Do not think that you can rely on your memory, however good it is. Having recorded the information, do check your cards regularly, to make sure you have missed nothing.

In these points, one to ten, I have assumed that you are going to visit the buyer personally, because in most businesses this is how you end up obtaining an order. However, I do not want to give the impression that it is necessary for you to start careering all over the country. A great deal of time and money can be saved by use of the telephone and/or letter.

Telephone

An initial telephone call to a company can save you a great deal of time and trouble. This does not mean that I am suggesting you change your initial telephone approach to the buyer – that still wants to be short and sweet. No, I am thinking about gathering information about a company BEFORE making an appointment. The girl who answers the telephone is very often a good source of informaion. Or, if your particular business is fairly technical, you could pretend to be a customer. Either way, ring up the company in advance of making your appointment and find out as much as you can. It could be that they simply do not deal in the kind of merchandise you have to offer, or perhaps they have a wholly-owned subsidiary which supplies it for them, and so they never look outside their own company structure. You should not need to travel hundreds of miles to obtain this information — it can be handled over the telephone.

That, of course, represents the negative side. On the positive side, you may well obtain information which will prove very useful in making your sales approach.

Letters

You may decide to send out a mail shot, advertising your product or service, to likely potential customers. A couple of golden rules:

1. Never send a letter simply addressed to 'the Buyer' or 'the Managing Director'. Ring the company first and find out the name of the man who is responsible for buying, and address the letter personally to him. Many letters marked 'Buyer' are simply thrown in the bin, without even being properly looked at.
2. There is absolutely no point in sending a letter unless you are going to follow it up with a telephone call. In salesman's paradise, a buyer would receive a sales letter and think — "Wonderful, this is what I have always wanted", and ring up immediately with his order. Sorry, but in real life, that does not happen! Your letter may excite interest, but buyers are not people who are used to initiating things. They are accustomed to just sitting there and letting the world come to them. With today's vagaries of the postal system, leave four clear working days and then telephone — your approach being that you are ringing to see if he has received your letter, and then whether you could make an appointment to discuss the matter further.

One final word — on the subject of customer entertaining. There is a lot of nonsense talked about this subject. It is a popular myth that salesmen enjoy enormous expense allowances and only obtain orders by bribing their customers with lavish dinners, night clubs and holidays in the sun. Like everything else in life, the buying/selling relationship is abused from time to time, and in some industries there is a certain amount of bribery. However, the vast majority of salesmen do not operate in this manner.

Asking your customer out for the odd business lunch is a good idea, provided you understand the objective. Taking a buyer out to lunch should not be considered as bribery, nor as a means of getting him drunk so that he will commit himself to placing an order with you — no, in today's pressured world, if you have details to discuss, it is sometimes far better to do it in a relaxed atmosphere. It is a great joy to get away from the telephone and the constant interruptions of the normal working day in an office. A pleasant meal and a few drinks in congenial surroundings will not only help you to get to know the buyer better, you will probably do more work than you would ever have achieved in the office. Bear in mind that the buyer who allows his purchasing policy to be influenced by how well he is 'looked after', is unlikely to last long in his job.

Selling is all about communication. Do not brag or bluff, or pretend to be something you are not. Be yourself. At all times show a lively interest and concern in the buyer and his business. Be honest, straightforward and efficient.

Yes, that's right — successful selling is common sense.

17. Do You Know Where You're Going?

The importance of sales forecasting.

Every business needs to prepare a profit plan in order to see where it is going. It is essential to try and gauge the future — you must be able to appreciate the financial and practical implications of what is happening to your business. A sales forecast is the essential part — the heart — of your profit plan.

Your forecast needs a great deal of careful thought and should be worked at in conjunction with whoever is involved in your selling effort — your sales director, agent, salesman, wholesaler, retailer, advertising agency — whoever is appropriate. What is vital is that YOU believe your sales forecast — it is a question of off-setting natural optimism against inbuilt caution.

So how do you prepare a sales forecast? Let us look both at existing businesses and brand new ones.

Existing Businesses

There are nine major factors which you should take into account in the preparation of your sales forecast:
1. Current sales levels — taking care to breakdown sales into identifiable product lines, departments, territories, salesmen — or whatever.
2. Seasonal patterns — being careful not to forget holidays. For example, Easter may have been in March last year, but in April this year.
3. Trends in the market.
4. The activities of the competition, and how it is likely to affect your business.
5. New products/services available and their likely impact on sales.
6. Scale of sales effort — advertising, salesmen, PR, mailings etc.

Are these being increased or decreased in the coming year?

7. Availability of supplies.
8. Production capacity – as it affects equipment, space, people and money. There is no point in producing a wonderful sales forecast, which, from a purely practical point of view, you would be quite unable to fulfil.
9. Resources in a fuller sense i.e. management time. Can your current management structure cope with the sales forecast?

New Businesses

Preparing a sales forecast for some new businesses can be comparatively easy. It may be that you are setting up in business because you have been promised work by a major concern, who could perhaps even be going to give you a contract. In this case, it is simply a question of assessing what other business you are likely to obtain in order to build a complete picture. Having done this, you should then consider the other factors I outlined for existing businesses, in order to finalise your plan.

Some new businesses are not so easy. Take, by way of example, a brand new retail outlet, shall we say, selling dresses. You have found your premises, done your market research, now you have to put a figure on how much you think you are going to sell in your first year of operation. Where do you start? The answer is to start backwards.

Begin by asking yourself what you have to earn in order to stay in business. Start with yourself. What salary do you need to pay the mortgage or rent and keep your family expenses paid? Then consider all the other factors – the business overheads, rent, rates, heat, light, staff, advertising, etc., etc. From this you will build up a picture, which for the sake of example, may mean you need to earn £20,000 a year. You will have already worked out what gross margin you are going to apply to your merchandise. So what turnover do you need in order to make £20,000 gross profit? Again, for the sake of example, let us assume it is £44,000. Having identified £44,000 as the minimum annual sales figure, then break it down. This means a turnover of £846 per week and based on a 5½ day week, this means £154 turnover per day. We will assume that the average dress you are selling costs £25. Can you sell six to seven dresses per day?

Armed with the knowledge that you MUST sell six or seven dresses a day, visit a few shops who are largely similar to the one you intend running. Choose shops in a comparable position to your own, in a town of about the same size and social pattern. Then talk to the sales girls and find out how many dresses they sell in a day. If the general concensus of

opinion is twelve, it may be that you can revise your plan upwards —
though be cautious, since you have to bear in mind that you are starting
a business from scratch. If the answer is three dresses, it could be that
your business venture is non-viable. In which case you should be
thankful you went through the exercise of preparing a sales forecast —
without it, you might have put your time, effort, and perhaps money
into a project which was doomed from the start.

There are so many factors which can affect sales and it is terribly
important to interpret the interaction between them. On the one hand,
sales may be increased dramatically by the impact of new salesmen, new
product lines, a new brochure, a new advertising agency — on the other
hand, these factors have to be weighed against cost — additional stock,
finance, office staff to handle enquiries, production staff to cope with
demand, space and transport. It is quite a balancing act!

Use your sales forecast, not only to plan the way ahead, but also as a
yardstick. Use it to monitor the performance of individual departments,
product lines, salesmen and territories — you may well be surprised by
what you find.

A sales forecast can only be that — a forecast. However carefully you
calculate the figures, something is bound to happen to alter them. It is
however vital to the successful running of any business. You must have
a plan and a goal — not only in which you believe, but also your staff,
your backers and your bankers.

In the compilation of our companion book, *Starting a Small
Business*, my husband Alan and I, had a long talk with a senior bank
manager, who is a particular friend of ours. We asked him if there was a
single ingredient which proved to be the deciding factor when he was
considering lending money to a would-be entrepreneur. Yes, there was.

"I go straight to the profit plan," he said, "and look at the sales
forecast. That's really the only part that matters. If I can be convinced
there are grounds for believing in that sales forecast, then I will back the
business. Overheads can be manipulated, problems such as premises
and staff can be overcome, but if the sales aren't there, there is no
business."

He is right, of course. So make sure that every twelve months you
wrap a damp towel round your head and spend a few days thinking out,
clearly and concisely, just what you and your business can realistically
hope to achieve in the coming year.

Overheads can be manipulated Staff/Premises etc can be Re-arranged - but if there is No Sales There is No Business.

18. Can You *Afford* A Salesman?

A step-by-step guide to employing a salesman.

I would like to suggest that first-time small businessmen should not employ salesmen. Far better to use agents, wholesalers or your own efforts, until the business is established. Salesmen are expensive and time-consuming, and even very experienced personnel managers will tell you that they have a great deal of difficulty in finding a really good one. However, for the purposes of this chapter I am going to assume that you have read very carefully what I have to say and that either it is not applicable, or you have chosen to ignore it!

Employing people is always a gamble. As most of us know from our own experience, it is very difficult to relax sufficiently to behave normally, at an interview for a job. There is however one distinct advantage in interviewing salesmen as opposed to any other type of employee. In theory at any rate, you will end up with the best man — since he is the one who has been successful selling himself to you.

There arc two types of salesmen available to you — the experienced or inexperienced man. With the experienced man you should expect to pay highly for his skills, but with him should come a number of very valuable contacts. There is no real limit to his age, though one would not expect him to be less than thirty and your primary concern will be where he has been and who he knows. The inexperienced man should be somewhere between twenty-five and thirty-five. The youngster is not ideal, since he may well need to sell to men in their forties and fifties and at nineteen, say, will experience difficulty in projecting sufficient authority. An inexperienced man over thirty-five, will find it more difficult to adapt to a career in selling. I feel, if he has had no inclination towards being a salesman by thirty-five, it is, frankly, too late to start.

What type of man you hire depends rather on yourself. If you have had plenty of sales experience, you may well prefer to train a young man to sell your way. If, however, you have never been involved in selling before, I would strongly recommend that you look for an experienced salesman — otherwise you are going to be in the position of 'the blind leading the blind'.

I am dead against using an employment agency to find staff. The vast majority are expensive and not terribly efficient, and you find yourself interviewing personnel who are completely unsuitable for the job. Interviewing is a lengthy enough process as it is, without your wasting time on unsuitable applicants. Instead place a classified advertisement in your trade press, local or national newspaper — whichever is appropriate. Do take care with that advertisement and make sure that you state all the necessary requirements, otherwise you will have a flood of letters from unsuitable people. State age, whether they need to be a car driver, the area in which they will work, whether you are paying a commission or a salary, or a mixture of both. State clearly whether the applicant needs to be experienced, and if so, whether he needs experience in your particular trade, or simply in selling. Then, do not give a telephone number, ask every applicant to apply in writing.

The first part of the sifting process can take place with those letters. Quite clearly a large number of them will be written by totally unsuitable candidates, for a variety of reasons — they are going to sit their driving test next month, they are seventeen but very mature, seventy-three but very sprightly, etc., etc. Neat presentation and legible handwriting are very important for a salesman. Remember, if the applicant is successful, you are going to have to read his salesman's reports week after week. "Ah", you say, "perhaps he has a wife who can type". Well presumably if he has, she would have written his letter of application. Clarity of thought is another important factor. In advising you of his background, has he dealt with it in a logical way? Is the letter pleasant, friendly and individual? Take time with these letters — you should be able to weed out at least 50%, if not more.

Now to the interview itself. You cannot learn much about a man in under thirty minutes. Yes, I know interviewing is tedious, but it has to be done properly, it is too important. The best way to handle interviews is to give yourself a clear day, with the intention of doing nothing else. This way you can concentrate properly on the job in hand. Here are some pointers worthy of consideration when interviewing a potential salesman: —

1. *Good, personal appearance* — sorry, all those sordid details like clean nails and dandruff on his collar. If you do not like the 'look' of him, then neither will your customer.

2. *Education*. Whilst a reasonable standard of education is obviously important, I would prefer, personally, for a salesman to have a fairly unspectacular education record, rather than be too academic. Top academic qualifications suggest he is a thinker, rather than a doer — it could also have the effect of making him a little patronising towards less erudite customers. No, what I look for in education is that he should be a good all-rounder. I would far rather he had a wide variety of very average qualifications, than an obvious bias in one direction or the other.

3. *Interests*. The same applies here, as with education. The wider his interests, the better.

4. *Health*. Being a salesman is hard work. He needs to be physically fit and you should ask for details of his health record.

5. *Temperament*. It is very difficult to reach the man behind his interview performance. Particularly today when jobs are so scarce, people are usually very nervous when attending an interview, and this can make them react in strange ways. Whilst you must obviously be sympathetic to this viewpoint, excessive nervousness with you, probably means excessive nervousness with your customer, if he is the successful applicant. You are looking for quiet confidence. Yes, all the boring clichés — a firm handshake, the ability to look you in the eye — these things do count.

6. *Marital Status*. I believe a salesman should be married. He is likely to work harder, and is less likely to plan his

sales calls round his current romantic interests!

7. *Ask him his aims in life.* If he is keen and intelligent he will have a master plan for how he sees the development of his career.

8. *Is he interested in your business?* Is he prepared to listen and has he done any research? Imagine for a moment that instead of your interviewing him, he was sitting instead in front of one of your customers. Is he listening to what you are saying? Is he thirsty for information about your business? Is he reacting to that information by pointing out his various attributes, which are particularly suitable for the job in hand? This is the way he should react in front of your customer.

9. *Honesty.* The best way to assess his honesty is to make a few provocative remarks. Establish his view on a topic, and then express the opposite one. If he drops his argument immediately and agrees with you, honesty does not come naturally to him. I am not suggesting you should provoke an argument, but honesty and integrity in a salesman are vital, and it needs to be established.

10. *Last, but by no means least, do you like him?* If the answer is no, do not hire him, however good his qualifications. This man could be vital to the future of your business and you have got to work together closely. You cannot do that if you do not like the guy.

Let us now consider the question of salary versus commission. Fairly clear guide lines are laid down, in as much that there is a 'norm'. Salesmen of consumer products are usually paid largely by commission. Industrial salesmen usually receive a full salary and no commission. Most salesmen are provided with a company car and out-of-pocket expenses.

The reason for the difference between consumer products and industry is fairly obvious. A salesman selling a consumer product – say, vacuum cleaners to electrical retailers, can very easily have his remuneration directly linked to his achievement. He visits a number of outlets during the course of a week and either makes a sale, or does not, and is paid accordingly. Commission is usually calculated on turnover.

In the case of the industrial salesmen, part of his job may well be the servicing of major 'house' accounts, which just happen to fall into his particular area. Very often in industry, technical staff play as big a part in the acquisition of an order as the salesman himself, and it could cause ill-feeling if the salesman was paid commission. Industrial sales very often take a long time to finalise and salesmen do have to live in the meantime. Also, since the orders are often very large, they frequently involve senior management in the negotiations.

On balance, I am not in favour of a commission-only salesman, regardless of industry. Although it seems a good idea to pay on achievement, without some form of basic salary, the salesman has no inbred loyalty towards you and your company. The pressure on him to achieve is great — too great. He will either panic and fail altogether, or start to use some fairly underhand tricks to achieve an order.

N.B. NEVER GIVE PRICE NEGOTIATION STATUS TO A SALESMAN WHO IS ON COMMISSION. HIS PRIMARY OBJECTIVE WILL BE TO OBTAIN THE ORDER, AND HE MAY WELL DO SO AT AN UNECONOMIC PRICE, RATHER THAN LOSE HIS COMMISSION.

The best mix in my view, is a good, basic salary, with a small bonus scheme linked to target achievements.

Before we look at what your salesman can do for you, let us look at what you can do for salesmen. Let us start with the practicalities. He needs sales literature, price lists, calling cards and access to samples and technical advice. A salesman works alone. He is divorced from normal office routine. He needs a great deal of self-discipline. If a customer needs to see him and the weather conditions are appalling or he is just going down with 'flu, it makes no difference, he has to be there. When customers have problems with your business, it is the salesman that takes the rap — he will be blamed for broken delivery promises and faulty goods, not you. Despite all this, he has to maintain a high degree of enthusiasm, and whether he does or not depends entirely on you, or your sales manager, if you have one. Salesmen are a hardy breed and can put up with a lot, but the most debilitating thing for them is poor management back-up. If he has faith and confidence in his management, there is nothing a good salesman will not do, and it is up to you to make sure he has.

One of the mistakes that many businesses make is to simply cast the new salesman adrift and expect him to instantly start bringing home orders. In the early days, he needs help from you, or your sales manager, IN THE FIELD. This should not look as though you are checking up on him — everyone hates that. You can say that you would like to spend the odd day with him, in order to see first-hand the kind of problems he is facing. When you are with him, watch carefully his performance with customers. Look for his strengths and his weaknesses, and after an interview, do not, whatever you do, jump on him and start telling him what he did wrong. One of the most vital component parts of a salesman is his ego. Whatever you do, do not start trampling all over it. He needs that ego intact in order to sell your merchandise. Discuss any shortcomings he has with him, but do not bully him. Make him feel the pressure to achieve is there, but do not overdo it. Above all, remember to congratulate him when he 'brings home the bacon'.

Now, what can your salesman do for you, other than sell your goods or service? Quite a lot. A salesman can be a marvellous source of information. The feedback he can give you from being out there in the field can be invaluable. Snatches of conversation and information he picks up, can help give you an overall picture as to the state of the trade and market trends. This in turn can help you decide future levels of production, stock requirements, etc., etc. Salesmen can also keep you abreast of competitors' activities – both their policy and their achievements. Credit worthiness of a customer is another vital piece of information.

Case Study

My husband is involved with a company which employs one particularly good salesman, who has many years of experience in the trade. He is a gregarious soul, with a genuine interest in everything and everyone. He was in the pub one day last year, having lunch with a competitor's salesman. He picked up the rumour that a major public company, with whom both he and the competition dealt, was having severe financial problems. He rang my husband straight away, and it was soon established that the business was owed over £30,000 by the public company. Despite the rumour, it was hard to believe that such an enormous company could really be in trouble, but the information was taken seriously. Five days later, when repeated telephone calls had failed to produce a cheque, my husband issued a Writ. Nine days later, he was paid. Fourteen days later the public company went into receivership.

Gossip – the ability to encourage it and benefit from it – may not be one of nature's loveliest pastimes, but it can be jolly useful.

How to control your salesman

Employing staff is an expensive business and if you are going to justify it at all, then you must work hard at getting the very best out of them. With salesmen in particular, you need to instil a sense of personal discipline, since their day-to-day life is fairly free from it. Here are a few pointers which I would strongly recommend:

1. It sounds obvious, but you need to ensure that your salesman has a loose-leaf address book, in which he keeps every scrap of information that comes his way.

99

2. *Record Cards.* As mentioned in Chapter 16, it is vital that a salesman keeps a record card on every person he visits, whether he has been successful in obtaining an order, or not.

3. *Weekly Sales Reports.* You must insist on your salesman submitting these on time, each week, carefully and neatly written, with full information on every day of their working week. You should suggest to your salesmen that these reports are completed on a daily basis, while their visits are still fresh in their minds. You should make it clearly understood that it is a requirement of the job that these reports are properly submitted.

4. You must insist that your salesman ring in to the office first thing every morning and last thing in the afternoon. He needs to do this for a variety of reasons — you need to know his itinerary for the day, so that you can contact him if you need to. You may need to give him instructions, or you may have queries regarding an order. He may need to pass through requests for samples or technical information. At the end of the day, he needs to check to make sure that none of his customers have been trying to contact him. Again, you must insist that he follows this procedure. Of course, from time to time, particularly in the evening, he may be involved with a customer and be unable to ring in, but this should not be a regular occurrence.

5. *Regular sales meetings are vital.* You need to strike a balance here. Your salesmen are only doing your company any good if they are out in the field selling. Sitting around, talking about it in the office does not pay their wages. I think the right balance is a fortnightly sales meeting — it is often enough to keep in regular touch with the salesmen, but not too often to disrupt their working week. Regular sales meetings are terribly important as a basis for an exchange of views, instruction and advice.

6. By contrast with the salesmen's report, it is also very important that you report to the salesmen on any changes or development within your business. It is vital that you make your salesmen feel part of the business and important to it. Out there on the road all day, it is difficult to give them a sense of belonging. Obviously, major changes of policy will be advised to them, but send them memos on more trivial matters, such as changes of staff, and keep them up to date on important administrative details, such as holidays.

7. Since industry first began, there has always been an element of

rivalry and mistrust between sales and production staff. Production staff believe that salesmen swan around all day, eating expense account lunches. Salesmen believe that production staff have no idea of pressure and plod along at half speed. On a regular basis, aim to get your salesmen and your production or technical staff (whichever is appropriate) together. Encourage a frank exchange of views — both parties will learn a lot and your business will benefit. Salesmen, for example, may be receiving a persistent complaint about some element of your product, or service. Only a meeting with your technical staff will jog their memories.

There are lazy, indifferent, dishonest and downright hopeless men and women around, who call themselves salesmen. Picking a winner is not easy, but find yourself an averagely good salesman, who is enthusiastic and caring about your business, and whether he succeeds or fails is largely up to you. There is a lot to be said for the view that a salesman is as good as the business he represents.

19. Do You Need to Advertise?

A cool look at the world of advertising.

I do not really approve of general advertising for small businesses, indeed advertising in any size of business should be treated with the utmost caution. Unless you are an enormous organization, purely looking for a brand awareness exercise, advertising should never be undertaken unless you are seeking direct tangible results from the advertisement you place. In other words, never place an advertisement unless you want something.

Never look at advertising as part of your major sales drive and never place an advertisement simply because you feel you should be seen to be advertising in such and such a publication. Trade papers are a particular case in point. A number of companies spend a fortune on advertising in their own trade paper, I presume in order to advise their competitors they are still around. Small businesses cannot afford this sort of one-up-manship.

Advertising is another one of those aspects of business life, which seem to be shrouded in mystique. Otherwise highly intelligent men become mesmerised into spending thousands of pounds of hard-earned profits on an advertising programme, which they seriously believe will revolutionise their business — and practically never does. The fault, I think, lies primarily with advertising agents. I have some very good friends who are ad. men (at least I DID) — they are not con-men, they believe what they say, but in my view most advertising agencies greatly overestimate the impact that advertising is likely to have. I am sorry to sound so unenthusiastic — of course advertising has its uses and we will explore these in this chapter. It is just that I am so painfully aware of how much money is wasted on unnecessary or fruitless advertising.

One final note of caution before thinking positive. Advertising can be very dangerous. Did you know, for example, that advertising can actually reduce sales? I read an article recently which confirmed that some years ago Ford motor company placed some advertisements in every other copy of the Readers' Digest. At the end of the year it was proved that the people who had NOT been exposed to the advertising, had actually bought more Fords than the percentage of the population who HAD. In another case, a brewery, who shall remain nameless, spent millions of dollars promoting a branded beer. After the advertising campaign, it was proved that consumption was lower among those people who remembered the advertising. Translate this sort of horror story into say local advertising to promote your shop, and you could be actually driving people away from it, rather than encouraging them. You do have to be careful.

Enough of the gloom. Let us now look at the plus points. Advertising falls into two main categories. There is the general advertising to promote a product, a service or publicise the fact that you require something. There is also direct response advertising, used by mail order companies, which requires the reader to actually place an order as a direct result of the advertisement. Let us look at the first category.

General Advertising.

Do not advertise at all unless you have something specific to say.

Perhaps you have opened new premises, designed a new product or service, are having a sale, attending an exhibition; perhaps you are looking for staff or an agent; perhaps you want to sell your company van, or buy one. You see what I mean? You need a raison d'etre. The first question you need to ask yourself is whether you are going to employ the services of an advertising agency (we will look at agencies in greater detail later in this chapter). If you are going to advertise on a regular basis, it is probably advisable to do so. If, however, you are a small business, wishing to experiment a little, why not handle it yourself? General advertising falls into four main categories:

1. Space taken in newspapers and magazines.
2. Brochures and sales leaflets.
3. Radio and television.
4. Posters, point of sale material and display cards.

Newspaper and magazine advertising.

You can prepare your own advertisement quite successfully without the help of an advertising agency. After all, you know a great deal more about your business than they do, and the newspaper or magazine will be only too happy to advise you on lay-out. Here are some pointers which are worth bearing in mind if you are intending to produce your own advertisement:

1. *Product research.* This might sound ridiculous, since you know everything there is to know about your product or service . . . or do you? You could well be in a 'wood for trees' situation. It is very easy to be so close to your business that you can no longer see the salient points. Talk to consumers about your business activities. Find out the points of interest, find out their prejudices and what attributes they think are important. Most vital of all, record the language they use. It is very easy in the placing of an advertisement to use trade jargon, which is perfectly understandable and recognizable to you and your colleagues, but not to your customers. Be very wary of this.

2. When talking to your customers, try and pinpoint the single factor that makes them most want to buy what you have to offer. Think about it, and above all TALK TO PEOPLE. Some weeks ago I had a letter from a company who had been advertising for salesmen to join their company. They could not understand it — with the country gripped by appalling unemployment, they had received virtually no response to their advertisement. They had advertised in the right place, their

trade journal, and wondered if I could tell them what was wrong. I am afraid it took me a long time to work it out. I stared and stared at the advertisement and its immediate impact was good. They stressed that the product they had to sell was well-known, well-established and probably the brand leader in its field . . . suddenly it came to me. They had given no indication as to how or what the salesmen would be paid − whether it was commission or salary, or a combination of both, and certainly not how much. I re-wrote the advertisement for them, starting off with a heading geared to how much a salesman could earn in a week. They re-advertised the following month and had two hundred and thirty replies.

3. *Positioning.* You need to decide where you are positioning your business in relation to your competitors. Research indicates that there is no particular advantage in saying that you are cheaper. What you need to do is to highlight some aspect of your business, which is particularly good. In fact your product may well be in a state of complete parity with your competitors in which case the added value will simply be that your advertisement states otherwise. It is a question of emphasis − if your competitors are concentrating on one element of their business, you might well be advised to highlight some completely different aspect.

4. *Image.* In the first section of this book we discussed the image − your business has a personality, just like people, and somehow you have to project that personality in the advertisement. Your product or service might be aimed at young people, in which case your presentation should be sharp and snappy. Alternatively, your image may be concentrated on quality, in which case your presentation should be classic in style.

5. *Whatever your image, your advertisement needs class.* Cheap, shoddy advertisements rub off on your product. Far better not to advertise at all than do it in a slap-dash way.

6. *Repeat performance.* If you are lucky enough to design an advertisement that works, repeat it and repeat it until its impact starts to pall. YOU will be heartily sick of it, but no one else will be, and while it is pulling, stick with it.

Brochures and Sales Leaflets.

You do not need to employ the services of an advertising agent or design studio, in order to produce a brochure or sales leaflet. These people are expensive – they can easily double the cost of a brochure – and in many cases their intervention loses the character of the business. What you need is a good jobbing printer. Work out what you want to say and discuss with him the lay-out. He will produce two proofs for you – firstly a galley proof, which is simply the type for you to correct, and then a final proof, showing the lay-out. Show this proof to colleagues, friends and customers. There will be a small charge for alterations but it is well worthwhile spending time seeking second opinions and reacting to them.

A word of advice on brochures. For the small business, use of the full colour process is extremely expensive and, quite honestly, not justified unless you are having at least ten thousand copies printed. You can achieve spectacular results with the use of one additional colour – i.e. black, plus one colour, which is referred to as the two-colour process. I have worked for many years with a small firm of printers in Manchester. The Managing Director had a stock phrase – "You can't beat red and black". Actually, I think he is right. Crisp white paper, coupled with black and red ink can have tremendous impact. Do not forget that the paper itself can also represent a third colour. It costs virtually nothing more to have a coloured paper, and the clever use of these three-colour options can produce a wonderful result.

So far as content of the brochure is concerned, the comments I made under newspaper and magazine advertising equally apply to brochures. Just one point though – do not be afraid of space. In a newspaper, space is at a premium, and you will feel the need to cram in your information. However, in a brochure or sales leaflet, the impact of your message can be greatly enhanced by a little space. Make it easy on the eye – short, sweet and relevant. Do not waste words.

Radio and Television.

Local commercial radio is particularly good as an advertising media for the small business. It is an unofficial view, but I believe you stand a better chance of getting your point across on the radio than you do in newsprint. Reading an advertisement takes effort on the part of the potential customer, you have to rely on them to turn to a certain page, and hope to goodness your advertisement is not dwarfed by a major news story. Not so with radio. If they are tuned in, the worst that can happen is that their mind goes blank! If your advertisement is that bad, then you should not be advertising at all.

With both radio and television advertising you need help from an advertising agency. Apart from the fact that such advertisements require professional skills, there is also the question of Unions. You cannot simply employ anyone to do a voice over on your TV ad. – in most cases they have to be a member of Equity.

Display Material.

I see very little point in the small business investing in posters on walls, buses, taxis, or underground stations. It is different if you are a large organization promoting a major brand name, but for the small business, the impact is so fleeting and the message so brief, that in my view it is of little value.

Not so with point-of-sale material and display cards. These, of course, are usually used in retail outlets for consumer products and are extremely valuable. Display cards carrying leaflets (you know the kind of thing the credit card companies use) can be a very useful advertising aid if placed in premises that your customers are likely to frequent. If you are selling your merchandise through a retail outlet, the supply of point-of-sale material in the form of display cards and posters can make a tremendous difference to its impact and therefore, its sales. This kind of advertising is fairly expensive and specialized. Again, I would seek the help of an advertising agency.

The success, or otherwise of advertising is difficult to assess, but needs to be judged on three levels:

1. The initial response, i.e. the number of enquiries you receive as a direct result of the advertisement. If the advertisement is successful, this should be approximately 0.2% of the readership, or indeed the viewing/listening public – whichever is appropriate.

2. You then need to assess how many of these enquiries actually turn into orders. Depending on how you have pitched your advertisement, the answer could quite easily be none. You may have attracted a casual response from people who have no intention of ordering your product or service.

3. Having calculated the number of orders you are likely to have received as a direct result of your advertising, you then need to calculate their worth, opposite what it has cost you to obtain them.

Direct Response Advertising

Direct response has one distinct advantage over any other form of advertising — because you are asking the reader/viewer to respond by placing an order, you can gauge exactly the success or otherwise of your advertisement in simple cash terms.

In theory, direct response advertising should be simple. You find an advertisement that works for you, match it with the media that works for you, and away you go. Not so, I'm afraid. There are so many other outside factors to be taken into account. Let me give you an example. Some years ago I was involved in a considerable amount of direct response advertising. The media that worked for me was the Observer. I placed an advertisement with a women's magazine by way of a test, selling T-shirt dresses. It was a huge success and an absolute sell-out. "Fantastic", I thought, "Now I can make a real killing. I'll put the T-shirt dress in The Observer. It has to be a winning combination". The Sunday the advertisement came out, the temperature dropped by ten degrees and it rained solidly all day. The advertisement was a complete flop. If it is not the weather, it can be the competition. I remember a couple of years ago, at the height of direct response advertising in the Sunday Supplements, seeing no less than seven pages of advertisements for digital watches, in the space of one magazine. Maybe their order response was not cut by a seventh of expectations, but I should not think it was far off.

Case Study.

A few years ago, a friend of mine, a director of an advertising agency, approached me and asked for some help. He had this wonderful idea. What he wanted from me was a copy of every direct response advertisement I had ever placed, together with details of the number of orders received, and what indeed those orders were in terms of size and colour. He had asked for the same information from several mail order companies, which he undertook to keep confidential. He had bought himself a computer, and he had the idea that by feeding our information into it, he would be able to come up with the solution to direct response advertising. It was agreed that when he had found the successful formula, he would invite all six participating mail order companies to lunch, and disclose his results.

About nine months passed and one day I received a call advising me of the time and location of the meeting. He gave us all an excellent lunch and half way through the meal rose to his feet, "Ladies and Gentlemen, with regard to the secret formula for direct response advertising, I have to advise you that there is none".

Yes, it is a gamble — take those T-shirt dresses — if it had been a heatwave that weekend, I would probably have made a fortune!

Let us look at a few golden rules for placing direct response press advertising:

1. Make your illustration as big as possible. Far better run just one illustration for maximum impact than a great many small ones.

2. Your banner headline must carry the price. Your price points are £15, £20, £30, £50, £70, £100. In other words, the general public are still as gullible as ever, and are far more attracted by £14.99 than by £15. Also, once your selling price goes over £20 you might just as well sell for £29.99, as say, £26.99.

3. NEVER SELL AN ITEM BY DIRECT RESPONSE WITH A UNIT VALUE OF LESS THAN TEN POUNDS — it just does not pay.

4. Where possible, incorporate a coupon to clip. This may be difficult if your advertisement is small, but asking people to write a letter to place their order, greatly reduces your response rate.

5. It is absolutely vital that you code your coupon, or if you do not have room for a coupon, that you asked the reader to write to a coded department. The only way you are going to build a successful direct response business is by knowing how each of your advertisements has performed. So you must know from where each and every order has come.

6. As with general advertising, if you find a winning formula, stick to it. It is tempting to say that if you are, say, selling electric kettles in the *Sunday Times*, that once you run an advertisement successfully, everyone who reads the *Sunday Times* has bought your electric kettle. This is not so — there are over a million people who read the *Sunday Times*. If your advertisement is successful, what it means is that your electric kettle appeals to *Sunday Times* readers. A certain number of them responded to your advertisement because they had a need for an electric kettle that particular week. It takes a long time to reach saturation point. If the advertisement works, repeat it and repeat it. A few years ago, during a particularly difficult period of strikes within the industry, my advertising agency made a mistake and I ended up with the same advertisement being repeated three consecutive weeks in a Sunday supplement. I was absolutely hopping mad, threatening dire consequences, which was not an

unjustified reaction, considering the advertisements were costing ten thousand pounds each! Luckily it was a tried and proven ad. The first week's response was excellent, the second week's better, and the third week's an absolute sell-out! I had to eat humble pie.

TV and Radio – Direct Response

This is a growing area, and again, as with general advertising, I would stress that in my view you should use an advertising agency. Direct response advertising, by TV or radio, requires a considerably longer amount of air time than normal advertising, since the viewer or listener has to write down your address and details. Because of this, some television companies are prepared to offer really favourable terms in order to encourage the direct response advertiser. I understand that with some products, particularly records, marvellous results have been achieved. It is, however, a very specialist area, and if you want to try it, find an advertising agency who already has experience of the media.

The secret to direct response advertising is to test and keep testing. Never commit yourself to an advertising campaign of any size, either with a particular media or a particular advertisement, until you have proved the formula is successful. Never for one moment believe that direct response advertising is a licence to print money. However good you are, you win some . . . and you lose some too.

A Guide to Advertising Agencies

Like everything else, there are some good and some bad. But unlike everything else, it is very difficult initially to differentiate between the two. The time most businesses discover they are using an incompetent agency, is when their advertising programme has failed – in other words, too late.

As I have already mentioned, if your advertising budget is small, do not use an agency, but once you move beyond the occasional advertisement in your local paper or trade press, you would be advised to use one. It costs nothing in theory for an advertising agency to place advertisements for you. They receive a 15% discount from newspapers, when placing an advertisement on your behalf, and this discount they keep. You are invoiced at the same price as you would have been charged had you placed the advertisement direct. However, in most instances, when using an agency to buy space for you, you are also committed to using them for lay-out, artwork etc., and this will cost considerably more than employing a little typesetter down the road. However, it should, of course, produce better results.

In selecting an agency, in my view it is important to find one which specializes in your particular trade. They know and understand the market, they know and understand which media are likely to work best, they know from the successes and failures of their existing clients, what type of advertisement is likely to work best. I would not be influenced by a location, or size — you need to find an agency that understands your business. *The Creative Handbook Limited*, has a list of all advertising agents, their address is *100 St. Martin's Lane, London WC2N 4A2*, and their telephone number is *01-379 7399*. They have agencies listed regionally. Try your local agency first (it is a myth that good agencies have to be based in London) and ask them for a list of their accounts. They will probably send you a prospectus.

Take time, and do not be impressed by the gin and tonics and rubber plants, and like every other area of business, do not employ them if you do not like and trust them.

    N.B. One very important point — in all your advertising do make sure that the statements and claims you are making about your product or service, are true to the best of your knowledge. False statements can leave you wide open for prosecution under the Trade Descriptions Act.

Advertising is vital to some businesses, totally unnecessary to others. Once you have a recognized business established, all sorts of people will contact you regularly with requests that you advertise in their publication. Ask yourself the same two questions every time you are approached:

    a) What is this advertisement actually going to achieve for my business?

    b) How many widgets or currant buns, or whatever is appropriate, do I have to sell in order to pay for this advertisement?

Expressed in these terms, most advertisements suddenly seem, what indeed they are, very expensive.

So think clearly and do not be taken in by all that jargon!

20. Do *You* Believe What You Read In The Papers?

The value of Public Relations.

Good publicity beats advertising, hands down, every time. Why? Because it is more effective and a great deal cheaper. A small business can benefit enormously from good publicity. It lends credibility to the operation and is an extremely cost effective way of advertising. Yet despite these facts, PR is often not even considered by the small businessman. So far as he is concerned, it is representative of the sort of window dressing used by large companies rather than a vehicle which can make a serious contribution to business development. It is readily accepted that PR has a role to play in building your business image, but good publicity can have far more tangible effects than that. I had a meeting a few weeks ago with a firm of PR consultants, who quoted me four case histories which demonstrate this point. Here they are for your consideration.

Case History No. 1

Their client, Anne, was a well-known outsize model, who worked over the years for most of the top fashion houses. Recently she retired and decided to launch a mail order range of outsize clothing. Her past experience obviously made her very knowledgeable about the problems outsize women face, both in terms of fashion and beauty. Having been a model, Anne is naturally gregarious and, of course, very good-looking!

So, rather than run the risk of an expensive advertising campaign, she instead decided to concentrate on PR. She tackled the problem in two ways, but with the same end in view. What she wanted to do was to gather a list of names of outsize women, who were interested in the fashions she had to offer.

Firstly, she approached a number of women's magazines and persuaded several to run a special offer garment from her range. You will probably have seen the sort of thing – most women's magazines offer, in each publication, a garment, a handbag, jewellery, etc., etc., at a special price to readers. How it works is this. The supplier, in this case Anne, actually sells her garment to the magazine at the sort of price she would normally sell to the average retail outlet. The magazine then increases the price to cover the production costs of the page involved and offers the item to the reader as a special offer. The profit the magazine takes is nothing as great as a normal retail outlet, so everyone wins. The reader has the opportunity to buy a cheap article, the magazine covers its space costs and the supplier is able to sell his or her merchandise without any risk of advertising costs. Special offers are particularly attractive to mail order businesses, as, in many cases, the magazine will allow the supplier to insert his catalogue when he despatches the goods to the reader. Anne has experienced great success with her special offers.

Secondly, twice a year, Anne goes on the road. She travels round the whole country on what is called a 'provincial media tour'. This means she speaks to women's page editors of local newspapers, radio programmes and local television. Different aspects of her business interest different people. She may be asked to talk on the radio about the difficulties of starting a small business, but at the end of the interview she can sneak in a quick word to say that if anyone is interested in her range they can send for a free catalogue!

Currently Anne has over forty thousand names which she has gathered purely by PR, and on which, when mailed, she can expect between 7% and 10% response, which is very good indeed.

Case History No. 2

Not all PR is concentrated on editorial, particularly when a 'brand awareness' exercise is needed to jog people's memory about an existing product. My PR friends have a client who produces bath additives. The Christmas period is an excellent time for selling this product, but, of course, there is a vast range of merchandise on the shelves.

Last Christmas, they organized a competition in ten key provincial newspapers, with circulations of over one hundred thousand, covering areas where the product needed a boost. Competitions are nearly always welcomed by newspapers, particularly if the prize value is fairly good. The competitions need to be very simple and the most attractive, from a newspaper's point of view, is where there are a maximum number of prizes. In the case of the bath additives, the company offered £150 worth of cash prizes per paper, plus a good number of runner-up prizes of product only.

The result has been extraordinary. Salesmen report absolute record sales in the areas where the competitions were run.

And just think, including the product prizes, the company cannot have spent more than £200 per newspaper, which in advertising terms would have bought them a space about the size of a postcard.

Case History No. 3

Sometimes PR concentrates on the trade press, every business profession or trade has at least one — usually three or four — specialist publications, and this can be a good way of introducing the client to new customers.

Our friends' have a client who is in freight forwarding. For some years now the company has advertised regularly in the trade press, with absolutely no indication of any tangible results. They had slipped into a routine of spending so much a month on advertising and yet, when asked, readily agreed that it was probably a pointless exercise. Our friends' persuaded them to cancel their advertising and they then studied the trade publications . . . and fairly tedious reading it made. They talked long and hard to the freight forwarders and built up a series of real life stories, of how they had helped clients in a crisis move their freight fast and efficiently. The stories are interesting — some sad, some funny, but they have two particular qualities:

a) They are extremely readable, and
b) the underlying message that comes across is that the freight forwarders concerned, offer a unique personal service, which is both speedy and efficient.

Their stories have been placed as editorial features in all the trade press and enquiries are flooding in.

Case History No. 4

Sometimes PR has nothing to do with the media! Our friends have a client who is a large provincial car dealer, selling predominantly second-hand cars. We all know about second-hand cars and the people who sell them — in our own minds we are absolutely determined that they are all rogues! Our friends' clients are not rogues. They run a smart, efficient business and take great pains to thoroughly check the cars they sell. But how did they put this image across to the local population?

Their immediate feelings were that they should launch an advertising campaign, stressing quality and reliability, but our friends said no, on two counts — one expense, and the other that sometimes a reputation can be better built not by what you SAY, but by what you DO.

Instead, they suggested sponsoring. It sounds expensive, but sponsoring local events, such as prizes at children's gymkhanas, swimming galas, 'keep our town tidy' campaigns and amateur dramatics — costs very little. Their concern with the local community, suggest that our dealers were decent people, and there was even a spin-off . . . all this sponsoring did excite a great deal of local media coverage. The result — a massive increase in sales.

You see what I mean? In each of these cases, there were some very tangible results from the PR campaign — a far cry from airy-fairy image building, it produced good, solid cash!

So how do you go about launching your own PR? If you are a small business, interested only in strictly local publicity, then, in my view, you do not need PR consultants. If, on the other hand, you are seeking national coverage, then I do think you need some help.

Handling your own PR

Journalists could do with some PR to polish up their image! On the whole they are an awfully nice bunch of people and surprisingly caring. Most journalists are only too happy to give some coverage to a small business, provided, of course, that the small business has something interesting to offer. The best way to make contact with your local newspaper is to go and see them. Firstly telephone the editorial department/sports page/women's page, whatever is relevant, and try and make an appointment to see the appropriate journalist. What the journalist will be looking for is some sort of angle to your business. For example, supposing you have just opened a local restaurant. The news in itself may not warrant any coverage, but perhaps there is some twist to your story. Perhaps the menu consists of dishes from your grandmother's recipe book. You have just opened a little manufacturing unit. There are plenty of little manufacturing units in your town, what is the angle? Perhaps you have landed an export order; perhaps you have made it a business policy to employ unemployed school leavers; perhaps your premises themselves are the story.

Try and make friends with journalists. Meet in the local pub — in that respect their reputation is entirely justified — most of them do enjoy their drink! If you are asked to provide some information for an article, make sure you submit it on time. If you are anxious that the article should not appear before a certain date, simply write the words EMBARGOED UNTIL 24TH AUGUST, or whatever date is appropriate. When submitting photographs, make sure they are black and white prints and make sure they are captioned. Try to persuade the journalist to state some practical information — their poetic licence tends to lead them away from the basics. Your customers need to know *what* you sell, *where* you sell it and *how* they get hold of it. When I was running my mail order business, I had the most wonderful editorial piece on the front page of the *Sunday Times* one week. The only problem was the journalist did not advise readers where they could send for a catalogue!

Local media is not restricted to newspapers of course. You will find local radio tremendously helpful and nearly always willing to interview you if you have something interesting to say. If you happen to have expert knowledge on anything which is of interest to the public, local radio always welcome a 'phone-in. It is a bit nerve-wracking, but you do receive a tremendous amount of air time. Also do not dismiss publicity on regional television as being too high powered and unobtainable. What is terribly helpful with all the media is if you know someone, who knows someone, who knows someone on the staff! As with everything really, personal contacts are a tremendous help.

Also, remembering our friends the car dealers, do not overlook local sponsorship. Even if your image does not need 'cleaning up', sponsorship still has the added attraction of bringing in plenty of media coverage.

Selecting a PR Consultant

The best way to find a reputable firm of public relations consultants is to contact the **Institute of Public Relations, 1 Great James Street, London WC1,** telephone **01-405 5505**. They will give you a list of PR consultants in your area, and will be pleased to advise you of the type of business each firm best serves. Like advertising agents, it is far better to select a firm who already have a working knowledge of your trade. Alternatively, all reputable PR consultants are contained in a directory called *The Hollis Press and Public Relations Annual*, which can be obtained from **Contact House, Sunbury on Thames T16 5HG,** telephone **09327 84781**.

Most public relations firms will ask for a monthly retainer, plus expenses. Compared with the average advertising budget, the sum involved is usually fairly small. However, a word of warning — do not expect immediate results. PR takes time. Time to establish contact with journalists, time before the articles are actually published and time before a gradual build up of exposure starts to have any tangible effect on your business. In my view, there is very little point in undertaking a PR campaign of less than a year, unless, of course, you are specifically wanting to promote one single event.

In order to get the very best out of your PR consultants, there are a few points worthy of mention:

1. Do keep your PR consultants fully informed as to all your company's activities. As explained earlier in the chapter, journalists are always looking for an angle on a story. Some aspect of your business development, which may seem comparatively minor to you, could make a wonderful piece of editorial. So do keep your PR consultants fully informed as to any changes or developments, however minor.

2. Provide your PR consultants with a good service. As with your salesmen, make sure they have up-to-date sales literature, and

samples. Journalists seem to operate in a completely different way to the rest of mankind. Having heard nothing from a newspaper for weeks, they will suddenly ring and say that they must have photographic samples, or a picture of the proprietor in three hours flat, for that night's edition. It is no good moaning about it and saying it is inconvenient. That is the way journalists work, and if you want PR coverage, you have to react.

3. Be prepared to give your PR consultants personal backing. Their best selling aid is you, yourself. Many journalists are simply not prepared to talk to a PR man, they want to speak to the boss. Talking to a journalist, or being interviewed on radio or television for the first time is a little daunting, but after a while you will find you become surprisingly professional! Be yourself, be friendly and relaxed, but make sure you get across the practical details.

4. If you are embarking on a national PR campaign, make sure that either you, or your PR consultants take out a press clipping service. There are a number of companies who specialize in this. It is their job, for a comparatively small sum of money, to ensure that they obtain a copy of every single piece of printed matter that is written about you. Similarly, if you are interviewed on radio or television, make sure that someone makes a tape or video. These, together with the press cuttings, can be tremendously helpful when selling your business concept to new customers, or indeed, potential investors. Have your press cuttings nicely mounted in a special book.

In the preparation of this chapter I had a long talk with John Hotchkiss, principal of the London based PR consultants, Hotchkiss-Kruger Associates.

"Why?" I asked, "is PR so valuable to a small business?"

John's view was this: "It lends credibility to your business in a way nothing else can. The British public, particularly, believe implicitly in what they read in the newspapers, and, by and large, they are right to do so. Our freedom of the press is probably second to none. This means that a product or service endorsed by the press is instantly a highly acceptable commodity, so far as the public are concerned."

He is right — it is all very well YOU saying your business is wonderful, it is a great deal more valuable, however, if SOMEONE ELSE says so.

Oh, and a word of warning — NEVER, NEVER believe your own PR!

21.   Do Your Sales Need A Cheap Thrill?

Sales Promotions — the pros and cons.

This chapter concerns sales promotions, which are specifically designed to increase sales in the short term for a particular reason.

Probably the most familiar type of promotion is the SALE, or stock clearance, where goods are offered at a substantial discount for a short period. The reason for holding such a sale is obviously that you have a surplus of stock, or stock imbalance. What you do have to bear in mind is that this kind of promotion contains some fairly substantial costs. If, for example, you have a retail outlet and have decided to hold a sale, there are three quite specific costs involved:

a)   The cost of loss of profit margin by offering discount.

b)   The cost of promoting the sale. You cannot simply say – "I am going to have a sale". You need to advertise in your local press, organise a leaflet distribution or perhaps advertise on your local radio.

c)   Cost of additional staffing levels. If your sale is to be a success, you will be inundated with customers, which you will not be able to handle with your normal staff.

Against these costs, of course, you have to offset what it is costing you to hold dead stock. You probably have an overdraft, warehousing costs and the increasing awareness that the longer you hold on to your stock, the less valuable it becomes. Again you are faced with a balancing act, but in these circumstances, I would look at the alternative option, which is selling off your stock through the trade. In every industry there are people who will buy surplus stocks. Their prices may be very low, but it is an option worth considering.

In addition to the sale, there are a number of other reasons why you might be tempted to run a special promotion:

1.   *A special line.* You may have bought in a very cheap line – it could be raw material or finished goods. You need to sell them fast, since your capital outlay is considerable.

2.   *Seasonal promotions.* This involves selling electric blankets in May, or bikinis in October. Strangely enough, because you are selling an item out of season, the general public assume that the discount is enormous. In a retail outlet particularly, a small display, indicating that the items are clearance lines, can produce phenomenal sales for a very small drop in gross profit.

3.   *You may wish to increase your order value.* Whether you are selling to industry, or to the consumer, 'something for nothing' always has an appeal. The idea that if you order a little extra, you will receive something free, can have a big impact on sales. However, do be careful how you do your costings. This could prove a very expensive exercise.

4.   *Encouraging visitors.* If you have a retail outlet, a restaurant, a hotel or indeed, anywhere the public visit, you might wish to run a promotion to encourage callers. A free glass of wine at a

restaurant or a 10% discount for first time buyers at a new shop. These added incentives can attract people quite considerably.

5. *Lotteries*. These are most popular among mail order catalogues. You know the kind of thing. If you order more than twenty pounds worth of goods within a certain period, your name will be put forward to be drawn in a lottery, where enormous prizes are available. I do not favour terribly this form of promotion, and certainly it has been criticized a great deal recently. In most of these lotteries, the odds against winning are enormous and once the public realize this, the promotion can actually cause resentment. Promotions are supposed to encourage enthusiasm in your business, not disgruntlement. With all lotteries, you do have to be careful not to break the law. There are some very tight regulations with regard to lotteries, and you should consult your solicitor before attempting to organise one.

6. *Presentation*. I am thinking primarily here of a retail operation. Good presentation makes it quite possible to promote an item without any form of price cutting.

Case Study

A few weeks ago, my husband and I spent a couple of hours in Tottenham Court Road in London, intending to buy a small portable television for our eldest son. We walked up and down the street – there is almost too much choice. We had practically visited every shop when we spied exactly the sort of television for which we had both been looking. It cost £159 which was about as cheap as we could expect. However, we decided to visit every shop before making our final decision. Two shops later we spied another television for £169. We both agreed that it was infinitely better than the previous one we had seen and decided to buy it. We were just about to make our purchase when a man walked in whom we recognized. He was the sales assistant from the shop with the £159 television. He began serving customers and we could not resist asking him why he had suddenly changed shops. It turned out he was the proprietor and owned both! When we told him we had decided on our purchase, he roared with laughter – the £169 television we were about to buy was exactly the same model as the £159 television two doors away.

"I do not understand it myself", he said, "At my other shop we had a surplus of these televisions, so we put them on special offer at £10 cheaper. We have left them at their original price here and we keep running out of stock. It is crazy.''

To cut a long story short he let us go back to the original shop and spend £159, but it still left us pondering. Why had we been attracted by the second television? Close inspection suggested presentation. With an item like a television, above all one wants reliability. A big display offering discounts suggests a cheap model. The display for the £169 television was discreet and somehow reassuring.

So display alone can promote sales – it is well worth considering.

7.   You will have heard of the term 'loss leader'. This is where a business sells an item at a loss in order to attract buyers, who, it is hoped, will at the same time purchase other merchandise, on which will be made a profit. This is all very well for great chain stores and supermarkets, but I really do not recommend it for the small business. It is a tortuous costing exercise and very difficult to calculate accurately, without a great deal of experience.

8.   The only type of sales promotion which attracts customer loyalty is the rather old fashioned cigarette card or gift stamp. These promotions were an excellent idea, but their appeal does seem to have waned of late. People seem to have less inclination to collect things. In addition, the same comments really apply as to 7. above. You need to be a fairly large organisation in order to administer this type of promotion.

In conclusion, therefore, promotions are a good idea, provided you do not let them cloud the issue with regard to what your real business is all about. Your aim should be to sell your wares at the right price in the normal course of trading. We can all sell goods cheap – it is easy – but if you are building a business, your priority should be to sell goods at a price which will make you money – preferably, plenty of it!

22. Should You 'Fly The Flag'?

A guide to export selling.

Finding an overseas market used to be something that had to be tackled by experts. Only if you had considerable experience in selling abroad could you tackle the export of your product. Not so nowadays.

There is a wealth of help and information available to the small businessman now, from a sub-division of the Department of Industry, called the British Overseas Trade Board. In line with most of us, I have a healthy lack of respect for most Government departments, but I must say the B.O.T.B. is the exception. They are very helpful, very commercial and absolutely red hot!

The B.O.T.B. headquarters are at **1 Victoria Street, London S.W.1**, or you can contact your local Department of Industry, who have regional offices everywhere, and can be found in your telephone directory.

If you have the time available, the best thing you can do is to travel to London and visit Victoria Street. There is an enormous library there, to which you have access, but most of the information is fairly long-winded and it would take you an age to research your subject in full. However, their great boon is the publication of a series of booklets called *Hints For Exporters*. These booklets are entirely free and are available for just about every country in the world. The details they give are so sensible. There is information on the customs of the country, exchange controls, trading hours, a synopsis of the economy, law and general legislation, hotels and their tariffs and even the cost of posting a letter. They also list the address of each country's Chamber of Commerce in Great Britain.

Having carefully read your *Hints To Exporters* booklet my view is that your next port of call should be the relevant Chamber of Commerce. Again, I think it is well worthwhile calling in person. The Chamber of Commerce concerned will be able to give you details of the agents, both in their country and in Great Britain, who handle your type of merchandise, and from there it is a question of going direct to the agent, and employing your very best selling skills.

The B.O.T.B.'s help does not rest there. They also run what they call the *Export Intelligence Service*, which at the time of publication of this book, costs £52. For payment of £52 you will receive one hundred and fifty pieces of information. You are given a questionnaire and you simply have to tick a series of boxes. The questions asked are the type of intelligence you require, the part of the world in which you are interested and the type of service and product you have available. As a result of this questionnaire, every time the Department of Industry receives an enquiry for your type of product, from the country of your choice, you will be sent the name and address of the enquirer.

If you are pioneering a market – in other words you wish to travel abroad to explore the possibility of exporting, the B.O.T.B. will send a form to complete. As a result of this, provided they are satisfied that you are carrying out a genuine market research programme, they will pay half your travel and half your accommodation costs.

The Department of Industry also assists with the sponsoring of overseas exhibitions. If there is an overseas exhibition of your particular trade, abroad, you can be sponsored to attend, and such costs as the building of a stand will be, at any rate, partly subsidised.

Then there is the Market Entry Guarantee Scheme which will provide 50% towards the cost of setting up sales facilities in overseas markets. This contribution is repayable by a levy on sales: if there are no sales there is no repayment.

I sound positively euphoric about the Export Market. Certainly, with the tremendous Government help available, plus undeniable opportunities overseas, it is a very attractive proposition. However, I have to say that for the small, and particularly, the new business, I would recommend that you first thoroughly explore the home market before attempting to sell abroad. Why?

1.   Selling overseas is extremely time consuming. Even if your agent is based in this country and you do not need to travel abroad often, there are still endless delays and a welter of legislation and form filling before you get anywhere near making a sale. Your business has got to support you, and possibly a family. You cannot live on fresh air. I would far rather see you establish a good, solid home market, which will pay the rent, before attempting to sell abroad.

2.   Selling overseas is still difficult if you have had no experience. If you are a natural salesman, with the prospect of a very good business opportunity, do not let your inexperience stand in the

way. But if you are uncertain of the market, and have had no export experience, it might be wiser not to attempt it.

Having said that, if you are going to try 'flying the flag' — well done and good luck!

23. Are You An Exhibitionist?

Are exhibitions a cost effective form of promotion for the small business?

If you ask most people to name an exhibition they will quote you the Ideal Home, the Motor Show or the Boat Show. Yet 90% of all exhibitions are in fact trade shows, aimed at industry and commerce, rather than the consumer.

Before even considering whether you should exhibit, I would just like to make the point that trade exhibitions are of immense value as a market research exercise. Assuming you are in an industry which does exhibit, not only do you have all your competitors grouped together under one roof, but incognito, you are free to wander amongst them, asking as many questions as you like. Just a thought — back to Chapter 1 — it is a great deal easier than tramping the streets.

Now to the question of your exhibiting. Without doubt exhibitions can be of tremendous value to the small business. Let us examine the implications on a step-by-step basis.

The Decision

Exhibitions are of value to you and your business if you have a product, or indeed a service, which needs to be seen and touched by your customer. Exhibitions bring the market-place to you, and they bring the right people. Compare, for a moment, exhibitions with retailing — the people who wander past your retail outlet are simply the general public at large. A great many have no interest in your product or service. A trade show acts as a filter. The people wandering past your stands are doing so BECAUSE they are interested in your type of product or service.

In my view, exhibiting should be just as cost effective as any other form of promotion. In some cases it can even represent the main sails drive. I met a small electrical component manufacturer the other day. He is not making anything fancy, just simple, straightforward products, for use by industry. His business was started quite literally in his garden shed, about ten years ago, since when it has gone from strength to strength, and is extremely profitable. He attends no less than eighty-three exhibitions per year. For him, exhibitions do not mean an opportunity to see and be seen. No, they represent his main selling tool for acquiring orders. This is the point really, just like advertising, exhibiting should not be undertaken unless you have a very clear idea of what you want to get out of it — namely, orders!

As part of the decision process, let us look at the costs involved. When taking exhibition space, there are two main elements of cost to be considered — the rental for the actual floor space and the cost of the stand itself. At the time of publication, floor space is costing approximately £60 per square metre. There is nothing you can do to ease the cost of the floor space, it is a fixed charge, but there is, of course, an enormous variance in stand costs. One point which I believe is terribly important – whilst, as a small businessman, you cannot be justified in risking a great deal of money on exhibiting, *if you are not going to do it properly, do not do it at all. In other words, I am dead against the trestle table stuck in a corner.*

There are three ways you can tackle the construction of your stand:

a) You can instruct a stand contractor to build you a stand, either to his design or yours. The costs of a stand can vary enormously, but range from two or three thousand pounds to over one hundred thousand pounds. So much depends on the degree of sophistication you require. However, as a rough guide, if your stand space was twenty metres square, it would probably cost you £7,000 to have a stand built – and bear in mind, at the end of the show, the stand remains the property of the contractor. It is not yours to take away.

b) More and more exhibition organisers are realising the value of encouraging small businesses, and at most exhibitions, you can rent a booth in what is called 'a shell scheme'. This represents a space, which is usually three metres by two metres, surrounded by three walls. I am sure you will have seen the sort of thing I mean – they are rather like a series of cubicles. The cost of renting a shell scheme for a two or three day show is about three hundred pounds, to which you have to add your internal fittings, such as display panels, lights, graphics and shelving, which will put the overall cost up to approximately one thousand pounds. Obviously, exhibiting in a shell scheme has nothing like the impact of having your own stand, but particularly while you are exploring the validity of exhibiting, this is a very good way to do it.

c) The third alternative is to purchase a modular display system. Modular display systems can usually be bought as kits, and they are usually represented by a series of panels and poles, which fit together in a variety of shapes. The good ones are lightweight and easy to assemble. The real advantage here, is that having made your initial cash outlay, the equipment is yours, and once you have established that your business is likely to benefit from exhibitions in the long term, it has to be a sensible move. If we take that same space of twenty square metres, the rental element will be approximately £1,500. To purchase a modular display system, which will make effective use out of that space, will cost you another £1,500. Because of Union restrictions, your system may have to be erected by stand contractors, who will also provide you with lighting, graphics etc., which probably will add another five hundred pounds to the bill. Therefore the total cost will be £3,500, as compared with £7,000, and £1,500 of that cost can in fact be amortised over a number of shows.

At the time of booking space at an exhibition, the organiser will advise you of reputable stand contractors, either to build you a stand from scratch, or to fit out a shell system. If you are interested in pursuing the idea of purchasing a modular display system, it is probably best to buy a copy of *Marketing*, where these systems are regularly advertised. *Marketing* can be obtained by writing to *Marketing Publications Limited,* **22 Lancaster Gate, London W2 3LY**, telephone number, **01-402 4200**.

As you can see from these figures, exhibiting is not cheap, to which you have to add the cost of staff time, transport and promotion – there is no point in exhibiting at all unless people know you are there. If, however, your product or service benefits from being seen 'in the flesh', as it were, then I think it is well worthwhile investing in a modest trial run.

Doing It

Exhibitions are not simply a service to industry, they are run by a team of exhibition organisers, whose intention it is to make a profit. You, as an exhibitor, are having to spend a considerable sum of money, and you need to see you obtain your 'pound of flesh' from the organiser. In the blurb you will receive from the exhibition organisers, they normally stress that they will be obtaining considerable PR coverage of the exhibition and advertising in various trade journals and newspapers. Try and take advantage of that PR. Before the show, go and see the organiser. Tell him your product is particularly interesting and you would like to be interviewed by any media that is around – with a bit of luck, he will point reporters in your direction.

Use any trick you can to encourage people on to your stand. Most trade exhibitions offer free entry, though entrance tickets are required. Send complimentary tickets to all your customers and potential customers, offering them a free glass of wine, or lunch on the house or whatever you can afford. MAKE SURE PEOPLE KNOW YOU ARE THERE.

In my view, not enough importance is given to the staffing of exhibition stands. I believe that at all times there should be a very senior member of the staff on the stand, who is authorized to make decisions.

I think it is perfectly justified for either you, or one of your managers, to be there for the duration of the show. Potential customers do not want to speak to some junior representative, they want someone at high level, who can give them some answers. If you are going to exhibit on a regular basis, then you probably need a member of staff whose specific job it is to attend these shows, but do not underestimate the need for a good man on the stand.

Obviously have a good supply of sales literature, and also a supply of forms for logging enquiries. On a busy stand, the last thing you want to do is to be writing out laborious details. You want a form with a series of boxes which can be ticked for speed and efficiency.

At all times keep your stand looking busy. We have all been to exhibitions where empty stands can be seen with the staff hanging around looking desperate. Even if there is no one at your stand, look busy and involved.

Follow-up Procedure

The enquiries you receive will fall into three main categories — those people who would like a specific quotation and/or samples; those people who would like further information in a general sense; and those people who have said that they are not interested in your product at the moment, but are willing to give you their name and address. Within thirty-six hours of the end of the exhibition every one of these names must have a piece of paper on his desk. As with the follow-up to a sales call, even if it is simply a question of confirming that samples are on the way, make sure you communicate. While the exhibition is still fresh in his mind, make sure the customer remembers who you are. There is little point in spending all that money unless every possible opportunity is exploited to the hilt.

In the course of examining the exhibition industry, I had a long talk with John Runacres, who is Managing Director of CLIP modular display systems, in Bristol.

"Is the small businessman justified in exhibiting?" I asked.

This was his reply.

"I have had years of experience in the exhibition industry and I have also built my own small business from scratch. I know how vital it is to make every item of promotional expenditure really WORK. I can honestly say that the exhibition industry has contributed enormously to the growth and prosperity of the small businessman in this country."

I agree.

Conclusion

This has not been an easy book to write because the selling and marketing of a business idea is such a personal thing. No two businesses are the same, any more than are two people. I hope in generalizing, as it has been necessary for me to do, I have nonetheless provided sufficient material in which you, personally can identify.

If there is one single message for this book — it is this. All the advice in the world is no substitute for your own determination to succeed. It is so easy, particularly in the early days of your business, to feel you will NEVER make it, and the most likely cause of your doubts will be lack of sales.

So — fifteen people in turn have rejected your proposal . . . what about the sixteenth?

Deborah Fowler